Educating the Next Generation

DIRECTIONS IN DEVELOPMENT
Human Development

Educating the Next Generation
Improving Teacher Quality in Cambodia

Prateek Tandon and Tsuyoshi Fukao

© 2015 International Bank for Reconstruction and Development / The World Bank
1818 H Street NW, Washington DC 20433
Telephone: 202-473-1000; Internet: www.worldbank.org

Some rights reserved

1 2 3 4 18 17 16 15

This work is a product of the staff of The World Bank with external contributions. The findings, interpretations, and conclusions expressed in this work do not necessarily reflect the views of The World Bank, its Board of Executive Directors, or the governments they represent. The World Bank does not guarantee the accuracy of the data included in this work. The boundaries, colors, denominations, and other information shown on any map in this work do not imply any judgment on the part of The World Bank concerning the legal status of any territory or the endorsement or acceptance of such boundaries.

Nothing herein shall constitute or be considered to be a limitation upon or waiver of the privileges and immunities of The World Bank, all of which are specifically reserved.

Rights and Permissions

This work is available under the Creative Commons Attribution 3.0 IGO license (CC BY 3.0 IGO) http://creativecommons.org/licenses/by/3.0/igo. Under the Creative Commons Attribution license, you are free to copy, distribute, transmit, and adapt this work, including for commercial purposes, under the following conditions:

Attribution—Please cite the work as follows: Tandon, Prateek, and Tsuyoshi Fukao. 2015. *Educating the Next Generation: Improving Teacher Quality in Cambodia*. Directions in Development. Washington, DC: World Bank. doi:10.1596/978-1-4648-0417-5. License: Creative Commons Attribution CC BY 3.0 IGO

Translations—If you create a translation of this work, please add the following disclaimer along with the attribution: *This translation was not created by The World Bank and should not be considered an official World Bank translation. The World Bank shall not be liable for any content or error in this translation.*

Adaptations—If you create an adaptation of this work, please add the following disclaimer along with the attribution: *This is an adaptation of an original work by The World Bank. Views and opinions expressed in the adaptation are the sole responsibility of the author or authors of the adaptation and are not endorsed by The World Bank.*

Third-party content—The World Bank does not necessarily own each component of the content contained within the work. The World Bank therefore does not warrant that the use of any third-party-owned individual component or part contained in the work will not infringe on the rights of those third parties. The risk of claims resulting from such infringement rests solely with you. If you wish to re-use a component of the work, it is your responsibility to determine whether permission is needed for that re-use and to obtain permission from the copyright owner. Examples of components can include, but are not limited to, tables, figures, or images.

All queries on rights and licenses should be addressed to the Publishing and Knowledge Division, The World Bank, 1818 H Street NW, Washington, DC 20433, USA; fax: 202-522-2625; e-mail: pubrights@worldbank.org.

ISBN (paper): 978-1-4648-0417-5
ISBN (electronic): 978-1-4648-0418-2
DOI: 10.1596/978-1-4648-0417-5

Cover photo: Khmer primary teacher and students in Phnom Thom Thmei Primary School in Banteay Meanchey.
Photographer: ©Mr. Chea Phal. Used with permission. Further permission required for reuse.
Cover design: Debra Naylor, Naylor Design

Library of Congress Cataloging-in-Publication Data have been applied for.

Contents

About the Authors	*xiii*
Acknowledgments	*xv*
Abbreviations	*xvii*

	Overview—Educating the Next Generation: Improving Teacher Quality in Cambodia	**1**
	The Importance of High-Quality Teachers for Economic Growth	1
	From Diagnosis to Reform: Three Policy Pillars to Raise Teaching Quality	7
	Bibliography	8
	Introduction: The Importance of High-Quality Teachers for Economic Growth	**11**
	Managing a Changing Teaching Force	13
	Using SABER to Diagnose Teaching Quality	14
	Notes	16
	Bibliography	17
Chapter 1	**How Attractive Is the Teaching Profession in Cambodia?**	**19**
	Key Messages	19
	Teacher Salaries and Education Spending	19
	A Comparative Analysis of Teacher Salaries	23
	Unpacking Earning Differences	26
	What Teachers Say about Salaries	30
	TTC Selectivity	34
	Entering Teaching	35
	Notes	37
	Bibliography	37
Chapter 2	**How Well Does the Cambodian Teacher Training System Train Teachers?**	**39**
	Key Messages	39
	Effective Teacher Education	39

	How the Teacher Training System Functions	41
	TTC Data Collection and Sample Description	42
	TTC Trainees	49
	TTC Trainers	49
	Classroom Observations	57
	Notes	62
	Bibliography	62
Chapter 3	**How Are Teachers Placed?**	**63**
	Key Messages	63
	Placement Process	63
	Placement Factors	63
	Placement Incentives	65
	Bibliography	68
Chapter 4	**How Well Do Teachers Perform?**	**69**
	Key Messages	69
	Teacher Performance	69
	Incentives, Salaries, and Teacher Placement	70
	Teacher Support, Evaluation, and Satisfaction	79
	School Director Behavior and Perceptions	85
	Quality Indicators: Teacher Capacity, Teaching Methodology, and Student Attendance	92
	Notes	103
	Bibliography	103
Chapter 5	**Teacher Outcomes: Mathematics and Pedagogical Content Knowledge in the Teaching Force**	**105**
	Key Messages	105
	Trainer and Trainee Mathematics Knowledge	105
	Teacher Mathematics Knowledge	115
	Notes	118
	Bibliography	119
Chapter 6	**From Diagnosis to Reform: Three Policy Pillars to Raise Teaching Quality in Cambodia**	**121**
	Policy Pillar 1: Making Teaching More Attractive	121
	Policy Pillar 2: Improving Teacher Preparation	124
	Policy Pillar 3: Encouraging Stronger Performance in the Classroom	127
	Bibliography	130
Appendix A	**SABER-Teachers Framework**	**133**

Appendix B	Oaxaca-Blinder Decomposition Methodology	135
	Gross (Unadjusted) Wage Differentials	135
	Conditional (Adjusted) Wage Differentials	135
	Oaxaca-Blinder Decomposition	136
	Note	137
	Bibliography	137
Appendix C	Tables: Teacher Wage and Income	139
	Bibliography	142
Appendix D	Scatterplots	143
	Bibliography	144
Appendix E	Multivariate Results	145
	Bibliography	150

Boxes

2.1	Teacher Standards in Cambodia	47
4.1	How Incentives Combine to Produce Total Teacher Compensation	76
4.2	What Is the Stallings Method?	97
5.1	PCK Item 7	110
6.1	How Singapore Attracts Great Teachers	123
6.2	Peer Collaboration: Japan's Lesson Study	125
6.3	Scripted Approaches to Encourage Student-Centered Learning: Escuela Nueva in Vietnam	126

Figures

O.1	Teaching Career Stages	2
O.2	Hourly Wages Are More Highly Compressed for Teachers than for Other Professionals, 2008–11	3
O.3	The Income Gap between Teachers and Other Professionals in Cambodia Is Much More Pronounced than in Neighboring Countries	4
I.1	Grade 9 Vocabulary and Math Performance of Enrolled and Out-of-School Children	12
I.2	The SABER-Teachers Policy Goals	14
I.3	Teaching Career Stages	16
1.1	Spending per Primary School Student in Southeast Asia and Pacific (Average, 2005–12)	20
1.2	Public Spending on Education in East Asia and Pacific (Average, 2007–12)	21

1.3	Budgeted and Actual Recurrent Expenditures	22
1.4	Hourly Wage and Its Dispersion—Teachers at Different Levels, 2007–11	22
1.5	Average Monthly Wage Income of Teachers and Other Professionals, 2007–11, by Region	23
1.6	Hourly Wage and Its Dispersion—Teachers versus Health Professionals, 2007–11	24
1.7	Monthly Income of Teachers as a Percentage of Monthly Income of Other Professionals, Cambodia, Vietnam, and Thailand, 2007–11	26
1.8	Hourly Wage Distribution for Teachers and Other Professionals, 2011	28
1.9	Recent Improvements in Average Monthly Teacher Income by Level, 2011–13	30
1.10	Trainee Self-Reported Grade 12 Exam Result, 12+2 Samples Only	34
1.11	Reasons for Entering Teaching, by RTTC-PTTC	35
1.12	Trainee Comparisons of Teaching with Other Professions	36
1.13	Trainer Comparisons of Teaching with Other Professions	36
1.14	Trainee Ranking of Easiest Aspects of Teaching, RTTC-PTTC Samples	37
2.1	Are Trainees Aware of Teacher Standards, and Do They Have a Copy?	48
2.2	Trainee Self-Reported Level of Preparation for Teaching, RTTC-PTTC	50
2.3	Teacher-Reported Problems in TTCs	55
2.4	Teaching Activities by Category	59
2.5	Time Use Segments by Lesson Period (1–3)	59
3.1	Trainee Priorities for School Placement	64
3.2	Teachers and PTTC Trainees on Factors that Influence Placement	66
4.1	Has Teacher Heard of or Received Good Performance Award?	75
4.2	Double-Shift Teacher Opinions on Quality	78
4.3	Teacher–Teacher Interactions	81
4.4	Does School Have System for Teachers to Observe Other Teachers?	81
4.5	Do You Agree that Hard-Working Teachers Receive the Best Teacher Evaluations?	83
4.6	Is Teacher Familiar with DoP Evaluation Form, and Have They Been Evaluated with Form?	83
4.7	Frequency of Teacher Evaluations using DoP Form	84
4.8	How Knowledgeable Is Teacher about the Evaluation System?	85
4.9	School Support Committee Roles According to Directors	88
4.10	Director Professional Development	89
4.11	Time Segments by School Location	95
4.12	Time Segments by Class Period (1–3)	96

4.13	Time Segments Using Stallings Observation Categories	97
4.14	Comparison of Time Segments in Primary Schools, TTCs, and Baseline Survey	98
4.15	Teachers and Teacher Standards	100
5.1	Knowledge of Grades 6 and 9 Common Math Items	107
5.2	Content, PCK, and TIMSS Averages	108
5.3	RTTC Trainee Mathematics Knowledge by Teaching Specialization	111
5.4	TTC Trainer Mathematics Knowledge by Training Specialization	112
5.5	RTTC Exit Examination Results by Specialization Area	114
5.6	Teacher Mathematics Knowledge by Grade Level	117
5.7	Teacher Mathematics Knowledge by Education Level	118
D.1	Khmer Achievement and Active Instruction (As Share of Total Time), School Averages	143
D.2	Math Achievement and Active Instruction (As Share of Total Time), School Averages	144

Tables

O.1	Summary of Teacher Mathematics Knowledge (Classroom Observations)	5
O.2	Class Time Use (Percentage of Class Time, Unless Otherwise Indicated)	6
1.1	Wage and Other Costs in Recurrent Funding	21
1.2	Average Monthly Nominal Income of Teachers and Other Professionals versus Minimum Wage in Garment Sector, and Income Growth Rate, 2007–11	24
1.3	Daily Income of Teachers and Other Professionals versus Poverty Line, 2007–11	25
1.4	Average Nominal Income of Teachers and Other Professionals in Cambodia, Thailand, and Vietnam	25
1.5	Mean and Standard Deviation of Selected Variables for Teachers and Other Professionals, 2007–11	27
1.6	Oaxaca-Blinder Decomposition of Income of Teachers and Other Professionals (Dependent Variable: Logarithm of Monthly Income)	29
1.7	Teacher Salaries, Monthly and Hourly Average	31
1.8	Covariates of Teacher Total Salary and Hourly Average	31
1.9	Teacher Payment Problems	33
1.10	TTC Trainee Salary Expectations and Difficulty of Entering TTC	33
2.1	TTC Population	43
2.2	TTC Descriptive Statistics	44
2.3	TTC Resources	44
2.4	TTC Laboratories	45
2.5	TTC Technology Resources and Policies	45
2.6	TTC Trainer Use of Teacher Standards	47

2.7	TTC Trainees	49
2.8	TTC Trainers	51
2.9	TTC Trainer Background and Education	51
2.10	Training and Work Experiences	52
2.11	TTC Trainer Salaries	53
2.12	Trainer Opinions about Training Constraints	54
2.13	TTC Trainer Interaction and Support	56
2.14	Attendance and Lesson Plans	57
2.15	Class Time Use	58
2.16	Teaching Materials (Classroom Observations)	60
2.17	Questions and Feedback (Classroom Observations)	61
2.18	Work Activities	61
3.1	Trainee Evaluation of Factors Determining Work Place	65
3.2	Trainees on Working in Remote Areas	67
3.3	Teachers and Trainees on Working in Remote Areas	67
4.1	Base Salary Index	71
4.2	Annual Unit Indicator for Base Salary	71
4.3	Positions in Each Grade	72
4.4	Functional Allowance	72
4.5	Monthly Functional Allowance for the Education Sector	72
4.6	Category for Pedagogic Allowance	74
4.7	Placement Allowance	74
4.8	Overtime Teaching at Secondary School	74
B.4.1.1	New Teacher Minimum Income with Incentives	76
4.9	Covariates of Teacher Receiving Good Teaching Performance Award	76
4.10	Covariates of Tutoring	78
4.11	Teacher Second Jobs	80
4.12	Teacher Observations by Director and DOE Staff	82
4.13	Director Knowledge of Teacher Standards	86
4.14	Working in Remote Areas and Placement Bonus	86
4.15	School Management Team According to Director	87
4.16	DOE Support According to School Directors	88
4.17	School Director Evaluation	89
4.18	Director Experience with DoP Form	91
4.19	Director Use of DoP Teacher Evaluation Form	91
4.20	Director Teacher Evaluation and Support	92
4.21	Director Appraisal of Teacher Quality and Incentives	93
4.22	Attendance and Lesson Plan	94
4.23	Class Time Use	95
4.24	Teaching Materials (Classroom Observations)	99
4.25	Questions and Feedback (Classroom Observations)	99
4.26	Work Activities (Classroom Observations)	100
4.27	Factor Analysis of Teacher Quality	102

5.1	Teacher Trainer and Trainee Mathematics and Pedagogical Content Knowledge	107
B5.1.1	Percentage Correct for Each PCK Item (7A–7C)	110
B5.1.2	Percentage Correct for Each PCK Item (7D–7E)	110
5.2	Exit Examination Results	113
5.3	Correlation Matrix for Exit Examination and Mathematics Test Results	115
5.4	Mathematics Knowledge Covariates	116
5.5	Teacher Mathematics Knowledge	117
A.1	SABER-Teacher Policy Goals in Cambodia	133
C.1	Wage and Other Costs in Recurrent MoEYS Funding, 2010–13	139
C.2	Determinants of Labor Income in Cambodia: Teachers versus Other Professionals, 2007–11 (Dependent Variable: Logarithm of Monthly Earnings)	139
C.3	Oaxaca-Blinder Decomposition of Male and Female Teachers' Income (Dependent Variable: Logarithm of Monthly Earnings)	140
C.4	List of Other Professionals Compared with Teachers in Cambodia	140
C.5	List of Other Professionals Compared with Teachers in Thailand and Vietnam	141
E.1	Multivariate Analysis of Student Achievement: Baseline Model Results	145
E.2	Multivariate Analysis of Student Achievement: Teacher Questionnaire Variables	146
E.3	Multivariate Analysis of Student Achievement: Director Questionnaire Variables	147
E.4	Multivariate Analysis of Student Achievement: Teacher and Student Attendance Observations	148
E.5	Multivariate Analysis of Student Achievement: Classroom Observations	148
E.6	Multivariate Analysis of Student Achievement: Teaching-Learning Environment (Student Interview)	149
E.7	Multivariate Analysis of Student Achievement: Teacher Mathematics Knowledge	150

About the Authors

Prateek Tandon is a Senior Economist with the World Bank Group. He has authored or coauthored four books on the labor markets, innovation, and economics of higher education, including the World Bank's 2011 flagship publication on the economics of higher education and growth. He manages World Bank investment lending to governments across the East Asia and Pacific region. He was educated at Yale University and Oxford University and was a Rhodes Scholar.

Tsuyoshi Fukao is an Education Specialist with the World Bank Group. He manages and supports education operations and World Bank-financed research in Cambodia, Myanmar, and Lao PDR. He was educated at the London School of Economics and University of Sussex and was a British Chevening Scholar.

Acknowledgments

The preparation of this volume was led by Prateek Tandon and Tsuyoshi Fukao under the overall guidance of Luis Benveniste. The manuscript was written by Prateek Tandon (main author) and Tsuyoshi Fukao. Jeffrey Marshall provided a significant contribution to the analysis of the teacher and teacher trainer surveys. Atsuko Muroga, Chandra Chakravarthi, Ravan Chieap, and Habtamu Fuje provided excellent research and technical assistance during the preparation of this manuscript. The task team is grateful to H. E. Nath Bun Roeun and the staff of the Cambodian Ministry of Education, Youth, and Sport for their advice and comments on an earlier draft. The final volume benefited from the excellent comments and advice of several World Bank experts, including Juan Manuel Moreno (peer reviewer), Michel Welmond (peer reviewer), Leopold Remi Sarr (peer reviewer), Lars Sondergaard, Beng Simeth, Franco Russo, Rawong Rojvanit, Enrique Aldaz-Carroll, Leah April, Sodeth Ly, and Juan Prawda.

Abbreviations

CESSP	Cambodia Education Sector Support Project
DOE	District Office of Education
ECE	early childhood education
ESP	Education Strategic Plan
GDP	gross domestic product
ICT	information and communication technology
IG	Inspectorate General
IRT	item response theory
LS	lower secondary
MoEYS	Ministry of Education, Youth, and Sport
NIE	National Institute of Education
OECD	Organisation for Economic Co-operation and Development
PCK	pedagogical content knowledge
POE	Provincial Office of Education
PSTTC	preschool teacher training center
PTTC	provincial teacher training center
RTTC	regional teacher training center
SABER	Systems Approach for Better Results
SES	socioeconomic status
SSC	school support committee
TIMSS	Trends in International Mathematics and Science Study
TTC	teacher training center
US	upper secondary

Overview—Educating the Next Generation: Improving Teacher Quality in Cambodia

Realizing education's potential to spur growth is a priority for Cambodia. By making education a cornerstone of long-term development strategy, the country's National Strategic Development Plan, Rectangular Strategy, and Education Strategic Plan have driven the expansion of access to education over the last 20 years. Net primary enrollments increased from 83.8 percent in 1992 to 96.4 percent in 2012, and net secondary enrollments from 16.6 percent in 2000 to 35.1 percent in 2012. And girls have equal access to educational opportunities.

But to ensure education's contributions to growth, Cambodia must tackle the next challenge of education reform: improving student learning. The 2010 Early Grade Reading Assessment of 24,000 students in grades 1–6 found that 33 percent of Cambodian children could not read and that 47 percent of literate children could not comprehend what they had read. Further evaluations found large performance disparities between urban and rural schools. Other recent national assessments on Khmer language and mathematics showed low student performance, with outcome disparities between poor and nonpoor and between rural and urban students. A recent impact evaluation found that grade 9 children performed at the same level in math and vocabulary as out-of-school children of the same age (Filmer and Schady 2009).

The Importance of High-Quality Teachers for Economic Growth

Education quality, rather than quantity, most accurately predicts economic growth. Increasing average education levels contributes to faster gross domestic product (GDP) growth only if schooling increases student learning—and the more the learning, the faster the growth (Hanushek and Woessmann 2008). Countries that achieve test scores higher by one standard deviation raise their average annual per capita GDP growth by more than 2 percentage points over 40 years (Hanushek and Woessmann 2007).

A high-quality teaching workforce—the bedrock of all high-performing education systems—is the single most important factor in improving student learning. Teachers, the largest element of Cambodia's education spending, are the most important determinant of school quality. Over a single school year, students with a poor teacher master 50 percent or less of the curriculum for that grade; students with a good teacher achieve an average gain of one year; and students with great teachers advance 1.5 grade levels or more (Hanushek and Rivkin 2010). A series of great or bad teachers over several years compounds these effects, leading to unbridgeable gaps in student learning. By upgrading its teaching force quality, Cambodia can raise student achievement substantially.

This study diagnoses Cambodian teaching quality and presents policy options for reform. Through classroom observation, assessments of mathematics and pedagogical content knowledge (PCK), and surveys of teachers and school directors, it sheds light on content and instruction, interactions with school directors, instructional support systems, and the implementation of teacher standards. It follows the stages of a teacher's career—entering the profession, teacher preparation, teacher placement, and teacher performance—and provides information on mathematics and PCK outcomes for teachers, trainers, and trainees (figure O.1).

The study seeks to answer three main questions:

- How attractive is the teaching profession in Cambodia compared with similar professions?
- How well does the Cambodian teacher training system prepare teachers?
- How well do Cambodian teachers perform?

Key Finding 1
The Best Students Are Not Attracted to Teaching
Teaching is not a particularly attractive profession. It does not attract Cambodia's top graduates: The grading system ranks teachers on a scale of A to f, where A

Figure O.1 Teaching Career Stages

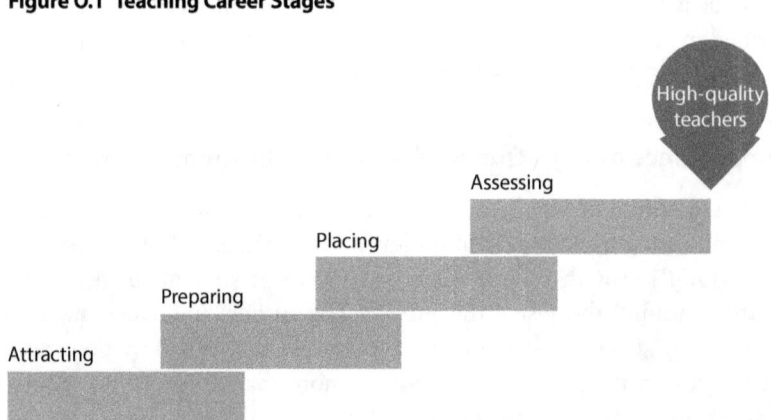

equals the highest and F equals failure; most teacher trainees scored in the E, D, and C ranges on the grade 12 exam. More than one-third of teacher training centers (TTCs) reported difficulties in recruiting qualified candidates and had a low caliber of enrollees. The lack of transparency in admissions has further lowered trainee quality. Entry requirements are not perceived to be difficult: year 2 teacher trainees believe that entering the profession is the easiest aspect of a teaching career. Raising the profession's selectivity and prestige is essential.

These issues are compounded by relatively low wages and a highly compressed salary structure (figures O.2 and O.3). The earnings of a married teacher with two dependents is below the poverty line. Analysis of Cambodia's labor market structure shows a noteworthy income gap between teachers and comparable professionals and also among teachers themselves, depending on gender and level, with prominent regional variation. But this statistically and economically significant income gap is not explained by differences in human capital endowments. In other words, the labor market is unfavorable for teachers, particularly female teachers.

Potential teachers care deeply about how their salaries will compare with those in other occupations (Boyd and others 2006; Dolton 1990; Wolter and Denzler 2003). Higher salaries attract better candidates to teaching careers (Barber, Mourshed, and Whelen 2007; Figlio 1997; Hanushek, Kain, and Rivkin 1999; Leigh 2009). And starting pay greatly influences how long an individual stays in the profession (Dolton and van der Klaauw 1999; Ingersoll 2001a, 2001b; Murnane and Olsen 1989, 1990; Stinebrickner 1998, 1999, 2001a, 2001b).

Figure O.2 Hourly Wages Are More Highly Compressed for Teachers than for Other Professionals, 2008–11

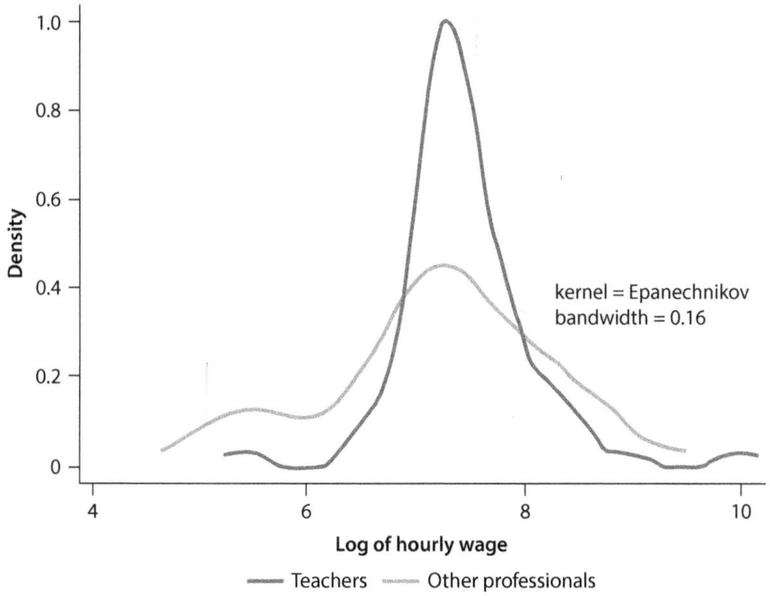

Source: Calculations from National Institute of Statistics 2008–11.

Figure O.3 The Income Gap between Teachers and Other Professionals in Cambodia Is Much More Pronounced than in Neighboring Countries

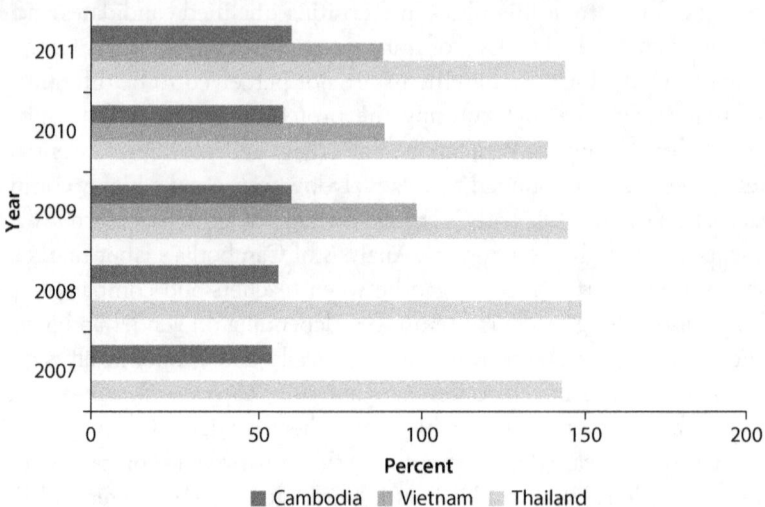

Source: Calculations, using World Bank 2012, Ministry of Planning and Investment 2012 (Vietnam), Ministry of Information and Communication Technology 2011 (Thailand), and National Institute of Statistics 2007–11 (Cambodia).
Note: Bars display monthly income of teachers as a percentage of monthly income of other professionals in Cambodia, Vietnam, and Thailand.

Cambodia's high pay compression, resonating with international analysis, has lowered the average aptitude of individuals who decide to become teachers. Severe salary delays and underpayment exacerbate the issue. Urgent reform is thus needed in starting-teacher pay, in pay changes over a teacher's career, in performance-oriented pay, and in pay delivery.

Key Finding 2
Preservice Education Is Not Delivering Graduates with High Content Mastery or Exposure to a Student-Centered Learning Environment

Despite adequate facilities and positive perceptions of school environments, most of Cambodia's teacher trainers have failed to provide sufficient content mastery and student-centered pedagogy.

Teacher standards, though officially part of the training curriculum, have not been integrated into TTC instruction, undermining their utility. Many teacher trainers have not heard of the teacher standards, and even teacher trainers with written copies seldom incorporate them in their classes. So there is a major disconnect between the Ministry of Education, Youth, and Sport's (MoEYS) teacher training goals, the stated curricular guidelines, and what is happening in TTC classrooms.

Teacher trainers also work in an environment with little contact, support, or collaboration. Their isolation—especially without well-defined mechanisms to assess training effectiveness, such as visits from the Provincial Office of Education—reduces opportunities to raise quality. And dictating lessons with little feedback or applied activities, or having students copy off the board for extended periods, suggests low-quality instruction. In only about one-third of classrooms did teacher trainees ask the trainers questions.

External measures of competencies show very low performance among both teacher trainers and teacher trainees. They score slightly lower than an average grade 9 Cambodian student on mathematics knowledge (table O.1). Trainees in fact know more mathematics than trainers (in all subjects). Many also lack the skills to diagnose students' mistakes and to propose solutions, raising concerns about eventual effectiveness in the classroom. TTCs must provide greater content and PCK mastery to ensure teacher quality.

Key Finding 3
Teacher Performance Has Been Inhibited by Ineffective Incentives, an Evaluation System that Is Disconnected from Classroom Realities, and a Lack of Opportunities to Learn and Share Best-Practice Lessons with Peers

Incentives do little to motivate top performance among Cambodian teachers or to raise student achievement. Many teachers are unaware of bonuses for remote/disadvantaged placement or are not interested because of distance and salary limitations. Bonuses for good teaching are widely awarded, but there is no evidence that they relate to teacher—or student—performance. Hampering incentive policies are perceptions that the bonuses are small.

Table O.1 Summary of Teacher Mathematics Knowledge (Classroom Observations)

Variable	All schools	By location		
		Urban	Rural	Remote
Content items	51.8	55.0	49.0	53.3
	(21.8)	(20.4)	(22.0)	(23.2)
Pedagogical content knowledge	55.2	52.5	57.1	62.2
	(20.7)	(21.1)	(20.2)	(22.3)
TIMSS	47.7	48.1	46.8	54.4
	(29.0)	(29.4)	(28.7)	(28.0)
Overall score	52.7	52.7	52.4	57.6
	(18.8)	(18.4)	(18.4)	(21.7)
IRT equated score G9*	484.9	482.6	484.7	516.0
	(96.4)	(90.5)	(93.9)	(122.4)
IRT equated score G6*	777.2	779.1	776.7	763.3
	(109.0)	(98.9)	(110.4)	(112.5)
Sample size (number)	671	138	481	52

Source: World Bank 2012.
Note: IRT = item response theory; TIMSS = Trends in International Mathematics and Science Study. Standard deviations in parentheses. All results are based on weighted data. For G9 and G6 comparisons, 500 is the respective scaled average score of Grade 9 and 6 students.

The teacher evaluation system is disconnected from teacher performance, teacher competencies, or student learning. The current MoEYS evaluation form, derived from the national civil servant form, assesses teachers on their merits as civil servants. If these evaluations are to motivate top performance and improve student learning outcomes, the form needs to be linked with the teacher standards.

Teacher support can also be improved. On the surface, the support system has many positive features: regular technical meetings, director visits to classrooms, and teacher satisfaction with their profession. But a more dynamic and collaborative working environment is needed.

External measures of teacher quality, including classroom observation and mathematics assessments, underscore the need to move away from teacher-centered instruction to more effective pedagogical strategies (table O.2). Mathematics knowledge is low—teachers answered only about half of the grades 6 and 9 mathematics items correctly. And the lack of lesson plans and student-initiated questions is a concern. Class time could also be used more efficiently, with less dead time or time off task.

Finally, much work remains in adapting teacher standards to the average classroom. Only about half of teachers have heard of the teacher standards, and about 25 percent have had them explained. Thirty percent of school directors have also not heard of them, and only about half indicated that the standards play a substantial role in the school's work.

Table O.2 Class Time Use (Percentage of Class Time, Unless Otherwise Indicated)

Breakdown by activity	All schools	By location		
		Urban	Rural	Remote
Class management	8.1	9.2	7.6	5.5
Get control	5.5	8.1	3.9	1.8
No instruction	2.6	1.1	3.7	3.7
Instruction activities	43.3	37.8	46.5	54.9
Teacher instruction	14.0	11.8	15.4	17.5
Students copying	15.5	12.1	17.4	24.7
Students reading	13.8	13.9	13.7	12.7
Recitation	19.8	20.8	19.2	16.3
Question-answer	16.2	16.7	15.9	14.3
Student asking	0.5	0.4	0.6	0.1
Student receiving answer	3.1	3.7	2.7	1.9
Work activities	23.2	28.1	20.1	14.7
Seatwork	14.3	18.4	11.5	8.6
Discussion	3.9	4.1	3.9	2.7
Group work	4.3	4.9	4.0	3.2
Kinesthetics	0.7	0.7	0.7	0.2
Sample size (number)	284	55	202	26

Source: World Bank 2012.
Note: All results are based on weighted data.

From Diagnosis to Reform: Three Policy Pillars to Raise Teaching Quality

Out of this diagnosis follow three policy pillars to reform how teachers are trained, maintained, and motivated. First, the government must make teaching a much more attractive profession. Second, it must improve how teachers are prepared. And third, it must encourage stronger classroom performance.

Policy Pillar 1: Making Teaching a More Attractive Profession

Attracting more talented individuals to join the teaching ranks requires a coordinated policy response, tackling many interdependent factors in a holistic manner, including salaries and salary structure, the profession's status, and TTC selectivity. If salaries and prestige are adequate to attract top graduates and if instructional quality is high, the TTCs will be able to impose stricter entry requirements. Conversely, without stricter entry requirements, the profession's status will not rise, even with more generous salaries. These interrelated elements require a harmonized policy framework. Reforms to be considered include the following:

- More attractive salaries
- Full and on-time salary payments
- More stringent TTC entry requirements
- More scholarships and financial aid targeted to high-performing secondary students

Policy Pillar 2: Improving Teacher Preparation

The low quality of teacher preparation and the isolation of TTCs from classroom realities prevent Cambodia's teacher training system from providing its graduates with sufficient content mastery and exposure to student-centered pedagogy. To improve teacher education, the government could do as follows:

- Embed teacher standards in daily classroom practice in TTCs.
- Promote peer collaboration among teacher trainers and the larger education system.
- Use scripted lessons to promote student-centered pedagogy in TTCs.
- Administer tests at the end of teacher training to assess competency and PCK.
- Increase the quantity and quality of real classroom exposure in the training.

Policy Pillar 3: Encouraging Stronger Classroom Performance

Teacher performance has been inhibited by ineffective incentives, an evaluation system disconnected from classroom realities, and a lack of opportunities to learn and share best-practice lessons with peers. Many of the policy levers for improving teacher preparation also apply to improving teacher performance, particularly in teacher standards and peer collaboration. But reforming incentives is even more urgent. To raise current teacher performance, the government could do the following:

- Ensure that teacher standards inform classroom practice.
- Promote further peer collaboration through strengthened teacher technical meetings.
- Improve lesson planning and execution, focusing on student-centered learning.
- Place teacher standards and teacher performance at the heart of the teacher evaluation process.
- Link incentives to performance and demonstrated competency.
- Create more effective incentives to work in understaffed and remote areas.

With a bold reform agenda, Cambodia can get the most from its investments in teachers and bolster student learning. Underpinning the educational investments that will drive growth, improving teacher quality is at the crossroads of service delivery, public financial management, and civil service reform. Almost every other sphere of Cambodia's education system has undergone a sea change of reform over the last decade. Teacher quality should be next.

Bibliography

Barber, Michael, Mona Mourshed, and Fenton Whelan. 2007. "Improving Education in the Gulf: Educational Reform Should Focus on Outcomes, Not Inputs." In *The McKinsey Quarterly 2007 Special Edition: Reappraising the Gulf States*. London: McKinsey.

Boyd, Donald, Pamela Grossman, Hamilton Lankford, Susanna Loeb, and James Wyckoff. 2006. "How Changes in Entry Requirements Alter the Teacher Workforce and Affect Student Achievement." *Education Finance and Policy* 1 (2): 176–216.

Dolton, Peter J. 1990. "The Economics of UK Teacher Supply: The Graduate's Decision." *The Economic Journal* 100 (400): 91–104.

Dolton, Peter J., and Wilbert van der Klaauw. 1999. "The Turnover of Teachers: A Competing Risks Explanation." *The Review of Economics and Statistics* 81 (3): 543–50.

Figlio, David, N. 1997. "Teacher Salaries and Teacher Quality." *Economic Letters* 55 (2): 267–71.

Filmer, Deon, and Norbert Schady. 2009. "School Enrollment, Selection and Test Scores." Policy Research Working Paper 4998, World Bank, Washington, DC.

Hanushek, Eric A., John F. Kain, and Steven G. Rivkin. 1999. "Do Higher Salaries Buy Better Teachers?" Working Paper 7082, National Bureau of Economic Research, Cambridge, MA.

Hanushek, Eric A., and Steven G. Rivkin. 2010. "Generalizations about Using Value-Added Measures of Teacher Quality." *American Economic Review* 100 (2): 267–71.

Hanushek, Eric A., and Ludger Woessmannn. 2007. "The Role of Education Quality in Economic Growth." Policy Research Working Paper 4122, World Bank, Washington, DC.

———. 2008. "The Role of Cognitive Skills in Economic Development." *Journal of Economic Literature* 46 (3): 607–88.

Ingersoll, Richard M. 2001a. "A Different Approach to Solving the Teacher Shortage Problem." Policy Brief, Center for the Study of Teaching and Policy, University of Washington, Seattle, WA.

———. 2001b. "Teacher Turnover, Teacher Shortages, and the Organization of Schools." Research Report, Center for the Study of Teaching and Policy, University of Washington, Seattle, WA.

Leigh, Andrew. 2009. "Estimating Teacher Effectiveness from Two-Year Changes in Students' Test Scores." Discussion Paper 619, Research School of Economics, Centre for Economic Policy Research, Australian National University, Sydney.

Ministry of Information and Communication Technology. Various years. *The Labor Force Survey*. National Statistical Office, Bangkok, Thailand.

Ministry of Planning and Investment. Various years. *The Labor Force Survey*. General Statistics Office, Hanoi, Vietnam.

Murnane, Richard J., and Randall J. Olsen. 1989. "The Effects of Salaries and Opportunity Costs on Duration in Teaching: Evidence from Michigan." *The Review of Economics and Statistics* 71 (2): 347–52.

———. 1990. "The Effects of Salaries and Opportunity Costs on Length of Stay in Teaching: Evidence from North Carolina." *Journal of Human Resources* 25 (1): 106–24.

National Institute of Statistics. Various years. *Cambodia Socio-Economic Survey*. Ministry of Planning, Royal Government of Cambodia, Phnom Penh.

Stinebrickner, Todd R. 1998. "An Empirical Investigation of Teacher Attrition." *Economics of Education Review* 17 (2): 127–39.

———. 1999. "Estimation of a Duration Model in the Presence of Missing Data." *The Review of Economics and Statistics* 81 (3): 529–42.

———. 2001a. "A Dynamic Model of Teacher Labor Supply." *Journal of Labor Economics* 19 (1): 196–229.

———. 2001b. "Compensation Policies and Teacher Decisions." *International Economic Review* 42 (1): 751–79.

Wolter, Stefan C., and Stefan Denzler. 2003. "Wage Elasticity of the Teacher Supply in Switzerland." Discussion Paper 733, Institute for the Study of Labor, Bonn, Germany.

World Bank. 2012. Teacher Survey, World Bank, Washington, DC.

Introduction: The Importance of High-Quality Teachers for Economic Growth

Realizing education's potential to spur growth is a priority for Cambodia. The country's National Strategic Development Plan and Rectangular Strategy call for creating a competitive economy through knowledge and innovation. To lay a strong foundation, the Education Strategic Plan (ESP) focuses on two key issues: achieving universal access to high-quality basic education and promoting equal educational opportunities to increase income and employment.

As a result, Cambodia has expanded access to education over the last 20 years. Net primary enrollments increased from 83.8 percent in 1992 to 96.4 percent in 2012, and net secondary enrollments increased from 16.6 percent in 2000 to 35.1 percent in 2012. Girls have equal access to educational opportunities—the Gender Parity Index for net enrollment in 2011/12 was 0.99 in primary, 1.13 in lower secondary (LS), and 1.05 in upper secondary (US). The early childhood education (ECE) enrollment rate for 5-year-olds rose from 24.6 percent in 2004 to 52.7 percent in 2012.

Cambodia's investments in human capital to promote growth follow development trends of the last five decades (Shultz 1961). Research estimated that each additional year of schooling increases long-run growth by 0.58 percentage points (Hanushek and Woessmannn 2007). Other evidence estimated the average rate of return of an additional year of schooling at 10 percent (Psacharopoulos and Patrinos 2002).

But new evidence indicates that education quality, rather than quantity, most accurately predicts economic growth. Increasing average education levels contributes to faster gross domestic product (GDP) growth only if schooling increases student learning—and the more the learning, the faster the growth (Hanushek and Woessmann 2008). Countries that achieve test scores higher by one standard deviation raise their average annual per capita GDP growth by more than 2 percentage points over 40 years (Hanushek and Woessmann 2007).

As Hanushek and Woessmann write, "economic returns come only from policies that effectively improve student achievement and that thus add to the skills of the labor force—and not from ones that increase schooling without improving achievement" (Hanushek and Woessmann 2009; see also Pritchett and Viarengo 2009).

To ensure education's contributions to growth, Cambodia must tackle the next challenge of education reform: improving student learning. The 2010 Early Grade Reading Assessment of 24,000 students in grades 1–6 found that 33 percent of children could not read and that 47 percent of literate children could not comprehend what they had read. Further evaluations found large performance disparities between urban and rural schools. Other recent national assessments on Khmer language and mathematics showed low student performance, with outcome disparities between poor and nonpoor and between rural and urban students. A 2009 impact evaluation (Filmer and Schady 2009) found that grade 9 children performed at the same level in math and vocabulary as out-of-school children of the same age (figure I.1).

A high-quality teaching workforce—the bedrock of all high-performing education systems—is the single most important factor in improving student learning. Teachers, the largest element of education spending in Cambodia, are the most important determinant of school quality. Over a single school year, students with a poor teacher master 50 percent or less of the curriculum for that grade; students with a good teacher achieve an average gain of one year; and students with great teachers advance 1.5 grade levels or more (Hanushek and Rivkin 2010).

Figure I.1 Grade 9 Vocabulary and Math Performance of Enrolled and Out-of-School Children

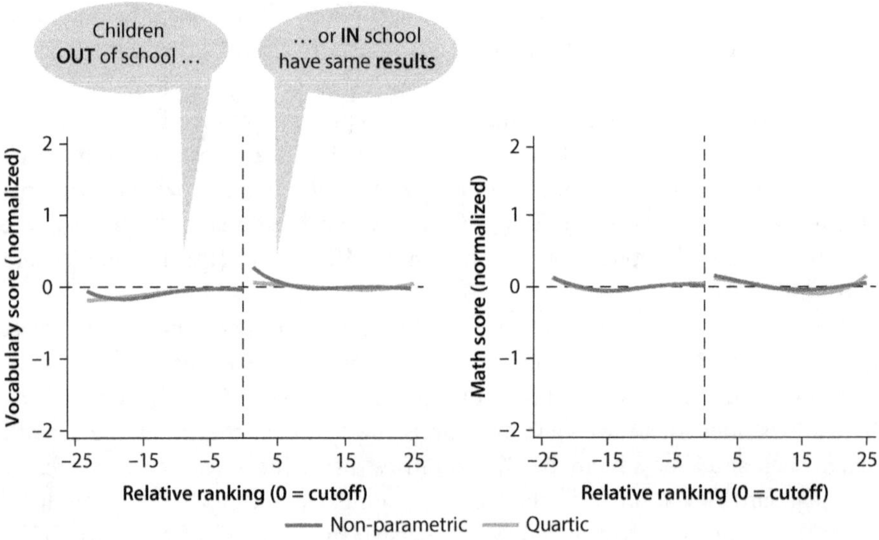

Source: Filmer and Schady 2009.

A series of great or bad teachers over several years compounds these effects, leading to unbridgeable gaps in student learning. By upgrading its teaching force quality, Cambodia can raise student achievement substantially.

Managing a Changing Teaching Force

"Teaching in Cambodia," a comprehensive study addressing Cambodian teachers, identified several weaknesses in teacher performance (Benveniste, Marshall, and Aranjo 2008). This study called for expanding the teaching force, reforming salaries, and delivering higher quality instruction by introducing teacher standards. It raised awareness of the need to review teacher policies, guided the government and development partners, and paved the way for establishing a subtechnical working group on teacher policy in 2011.

This study informed the government as it managed an expanding teaching force. Today there are 83,051 public school teachers in Cambodia, 10 percent more than in 2007: 44,840 primary; 27,054 LS; and 11,157 US. The numbers of LS and US teachers rose by 30 percent and 65 percent, respectively.[1] In 2012, 70 percent of the teaching force was employed in rural schools, 25 percent in urban schools, and 5 percent in remote schools.[2]

This expansion resulted from an increase in teacher training center (TTC) graduates from 3,700 in 2006 to about 5,000 today. Of these new teachers, 200 are in ECE; 2,100 in primary; 1,500 in LS; 1,000 in US; 50 in higher education; and 150 in sport. With approximately 1,500 retirements and 1,000 turnovers every year, the average annual increase in the stock of teachers is 2,500. But teacher-student ratios remain high in early education: the 2013 primary teacher-student ratio is 48.3, from 51.3 in 2007. LS and US ratios improved to 19.8 and 25.9, respectively, in 2013—a marked contrast from 30.6 and 33.2 in 2007.

Teachers' education levels also rose substantially, particularly among the younger generation. In 2013 more than half of primary school teachers held an US degree or higher, compared with only one-quarter in 2007. Over 80 percent of secondary teachers had completed at least grade 12, up from 65 percent in 2007. Today, two-thirds of teachers hold an US degree or higher. But the qualifications of teachers in rural and remote schools lag behind those of their urban counterparts. Most primary school teachers who have completed only grade 9 work in remote schools. Most who have completed grade 12 work in urban schools.

The teaching profession remains male dominated, although the gender gap has been narrowing. Female teachers now account for 44 percent of the teaching force, up from 39 percent in 2007. Their numbers have risen particularly in primary (42–49 percent) and LS (33–42 percent). But only 10 percent of school directors are female. More than half of Cambodian teachers are under 40; 57–69 percent of teachers in remote areas are under 30.

New strategies to address primary teacher shortages in rural areas have expanded over the last several years. One-quarter (11,776) of primary teachers taught double shifts in 2011. Most of these teachers work in rural areas; urban primary teachers usually prefer more lucrative opportunities such as private tutoring. Multigrade teaching—instructing two or three grades during the same class session—has almost doubled since 2007. Five percent (2,464) of primary teachers taught multigrades in 2011, mostly in rural and remote areas.

Using SABER to Diagnose Teaching Quality

The World Bank's Systems Approach for Better Education Results (SABER) initiative conducted a teacher policy analysis for Cambodia in 2012 in accordance with its SABER-Teachers framework (figure I.2).[3]

The 2012 SABER analysis (appendix table A.1) suggested three areas for further investigation: making teaching a more attractive profession; improving teacher preparation; and improving classroom instruction.

This study focuses on these three dimensions, examining not only teacher training and capacity, but also how teachers deliver instruction and interact with students. We identify the main constraints to improving performance and showcase how other countries have addressed these challenges. Using classroom surveys and the latest evidence from the labor market, we investigate how to improve the teaching system to produce better student learning outcomes.

Figure I.2 The SABER-Teachers Policy Goals

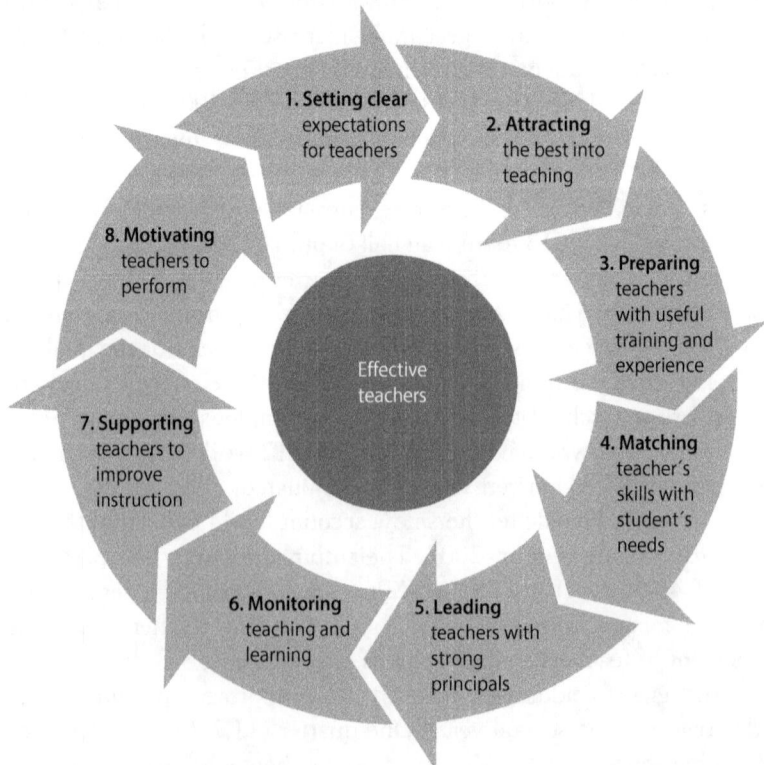

We seek to answer three main questions:

- How attractive is the teaching profession in Cambodia?
- How well does the Cambodian teacher training system prepare teachers?
- How well do Cambodian teachers perform?

The answers to these questions derive primarily from two surveys of teachers and teachers-in-training carried out in late 2012 and early 2013. These surveys followed the 2008 study's direct classroom observation method, based on the time-on-task and time segment studies pioneered by Bloom, Dunn, and Morse (1964) and Stallings and Kaskowitz (1974). The observation instruments, divided into five areas representing the most common in-class activities (instruction, recitation, and so forth), allow us to describe a class through its activities and evolution from start to finish. At 15-second intervals, the enumerator marks the box that best describes the activity undertaken at that moment. These marks are then aggregated by segment and area and then divided by the total to create a percentage breakdown of time spent in each activity.

Through classroom observation data, mathematics and pedagogical content knowledge (PCK) assessments, and surveys of teachers and school directors, we also shed light on content and instruction, interactions with school directors, instructional support, and the implementation of teacher standards. The full set of primary data sources is as follows:

- Cambodia's Education Management Information System provides yearly detailed data of education inputs and outputs for each school from 1998 to 2012.

- The 2007–11 Cambodia Socio-Economic Surveys (National Institutes of Statistics various years) include occupational and wage information for teachers and other professionals. The surveys' large sample sizes (over 51,000 people per survey, 70 percent of whom are ages 15–64) allow for numerous teacher interviews (an average of 559 per year).

- The 2012 Teacher Training Center Survey (World Bank 2012a) collected data on 10 of 24 TTCs nationwide, covering approximately 102 trainers and 952 trainees. It includes descriptive information on schools' physical condition, a trainer and trainee questionnaire, TTC classroom observation, and assessments of mathematics and PCK for trainers and trainees. In each TTC, the data were collected during a three-day visit. It includes information from 10 TTC director surveys; 20 classroom observations (10 math classes, 9 Khmer classes, and 1 history class); 102 trainer surveys and completed sample tests of math and PCK; and 952 trainee surveys and completed sample tests of math and PCK.

- The Teacher Policy Survey (World Bank 2012b), carried out between October 2012 and June 2013, collected data on 150 primary schools in all 24 provinces.

Figure I.3 Teaching Career Stages

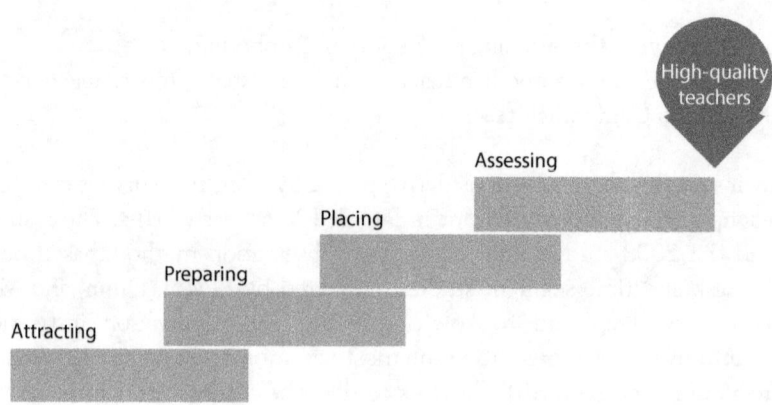

In each school, trained teams of enumerators spent two days conducting surveys for teachers, directors, and community representatives and administering sample tests of PCK and mathematics for teachers. The Teacher Policy Survey also included classroom observations, focusing on teacher preparation and teaching methods. The teams surveyed 149 school directors and 676 teachers; reviewed 150 teacher and student attendance forms; observed 284 classrooms (grade 3 math and Khmer classes); interviewed 534 community representatives; and conducted math and PCK assessments for 689 teachers. Enumerators also collected data on teacher preparation before the classroom observation.

This study follows the stages of a teaching career—decision to enter the profession, teacher preparation, teacher placement, and teacher performance—and provides information on mathematics and PCK outcomes for teachers, trainers, and trainees (figure I.3).

Notes

1. Education Management Information System.
2. Human Resource Management Information System.
3. Developed in 2011, the SABER-Teachers tool catalyzes and informs dialogue on policies to improve teaching quality. SABER's eight crucial teacher development policy goals (figure I.2) are as follows:
   - Setting requirements for entering and remaining in the teaching profession
   - Ensuring that (a) private and public teacher institutions function at acceptable standards in curriculum, teachers, facilities, organization, and the follow-up of graduates and (b) teacher trainees acquire sufficient subject knowledge and teaching practice
   - Establishing recruitment and employment practices to ensure that teacher skills meet student needs
   - Rewarding high-performing teachers with salary and nonsalary benefits

- Setting rules, policies, and procedures for professional development, including support for beginning teachers
- Monitoring and evaluating teacher quality
- Bolstering school leadership by recruiting, evaluating, rewarding and sanctioning school principals

In SABER, education systems are classified as more or less advanced in each of these goals. The four classifications are latent, emerging, established, and advanced. The SABER ratings refer to whether teacher policies are in place. No analysis of implementation was done.

Bibliography

Benveniste, Luis, Jeffery Marshall, and M. Caridad Aranjo. 2008. *Teaching in Cambodia*. Washington, DC: World Bank.

Bloom, Richard, James A. Dunn, and William C. Morse. 1964. "Data-Source Consensus: A Fundamental Problem in Classroom Research." *Journal of Educational Measurement* 1 (2): 119–23.

Cambodia Administrative Reform General Secretariat 2010. "Human Resource Management Information System." Government of Cambodia, Phnom Penh.

Education Management Information System. Ministry of Education, Youth, and Sports. Government of Cambodia.

Filmer, Deon, and Norbert Schady 2009. "School Enrollment, Selection and Test Scores," Policy Research Working Paper 4998, World Bank, Washington, DC.

Hanushek, Eric A., and Ludger Woessmannn. 2007. "The Role of Education Quality in Economic Growth." Policy Research Working Paper 4122, World Bank, Washington, DC.

———. 2008. "The Role of Cognitive Skills in Economic Development." *Journal of Economic Literature* 46 (3): 607–88.

Hanushek, Eric A., and Steven G. Rivkin. 2010. "Generalizations about Using Value-Added Measures of Teacher Quality." *American Economic Review* 100 (2): 267–71.

IMF (International Monetary Fund). 2012. Cambodia: 2011 Article IV Consultation. Country Report 12/46, IMF, Washington, DC.

National Institute of Statistics. Various years. *Cambodia Socio-Economic Survey*. Phnom Penh: Royal Government of Cambodia, Ministry of Planning.

Psacharopoulos, George, and Anthony H. Patrinos. 2002. "Returns to Investment in Education: A Further Update." Policy Research Working Paper 2881, World Bank, Washington, DC.

Ministry of Education, Youth, and Sports. Education Master Plan draft. 2010 and 2014.

Ministry of Information and Communication Technology. Various years. *The Labor Force Survey*. Bangkok: National Statistical Office.

Ministry of Planning and Investment. Various years. *The Labor Force Survey*. Hanoi: General Statistics Office.

Stallings, Jane A., and David H. Kaskowitz. 1974. *Follow Through Classroom Observation Evaluation 1972–1973*. SRI Project URU-7370. Menlo Park, CA: Stanford Research Institute.

Theodore W. Schultz. 1961. "Investment in Human Capital." *American Economic Review* 51 (1): 1–17.

UNESCO (United Nations Educational, Scientific and Cultural Organization). 2006. *Teachers and Educational Quality: Monitoring Global Needs for 2015*. Montreal: Institute for Statistics.

UNESCAP (United Nations Economic and Social Commission for Asia and Pacific). 2012. *Traders Manual for Least Developed Countries: Cambodia*. New York: United Nations.

World Bank. 2009. "Education at a Glance: Cambodia." Washington, DC.

———. 2012. *World Development Indicators 2012*. Washington, DC.

CHAPTER 1

How Attractive Is the Teaching Profession in Cambodia?

Key Messages

Teacher wages are low. The wages of a typical married Cambodian teacher with two children are below the poverty line. The income gap is substantial between teachers and other professionals. And even when controlling for human capital endowments, teachers—particularly female teachers—suffer from systematic labor market disadvantage compared with other Cambodian professionals.

High salary compression is also undermining teaching's attractiveness as a career and limiting its ability to attract great candidates. Urgent reform is needed in starting-teacher pay, in pay changes over a teacher's career, in performance-oriented pay, and in pay delivery.

Although teachers in service have favorable impressions of their working conditions, teaching does not attract Cambodia's top graduates. The majority of teacher training center (TTC) applicants score in the bottom range of the grade 12 exit examination. TTCs report difficulties in recruiting qualified candidates and dissatisfaction with enrollee caliber. Entry requirements are also not considered difficult, indicating teaching's low prestige.

Teacher Salaries and Education Spending

Attracting the best individuals into teaching requires competitive pay and consideration of entry requirements and working conditions. We touch on these issues in this chapter, beginning with a review of the government's education spending to provide context.

The government has committed to increasing the education budget and teachers' pay in recent years. In 2010, it increased education spending to 17.8 percent of recurrent government expenditure, and it plans a further increase in 2014 (MoEYS 2010). Primary education accounts for 64.5 percent of education spending, and secondary education for 11.2 percent (World Bank 2009). But primary education spending per student as a percentage of gross domestic product (GDP) per capita is lower than in other countries in the region (figure 1.1).

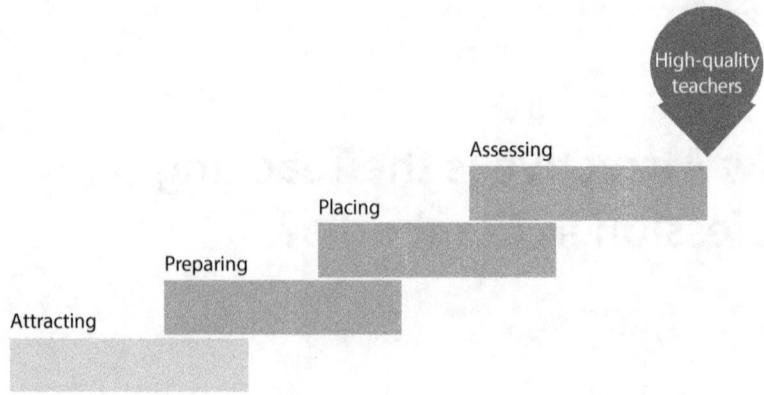

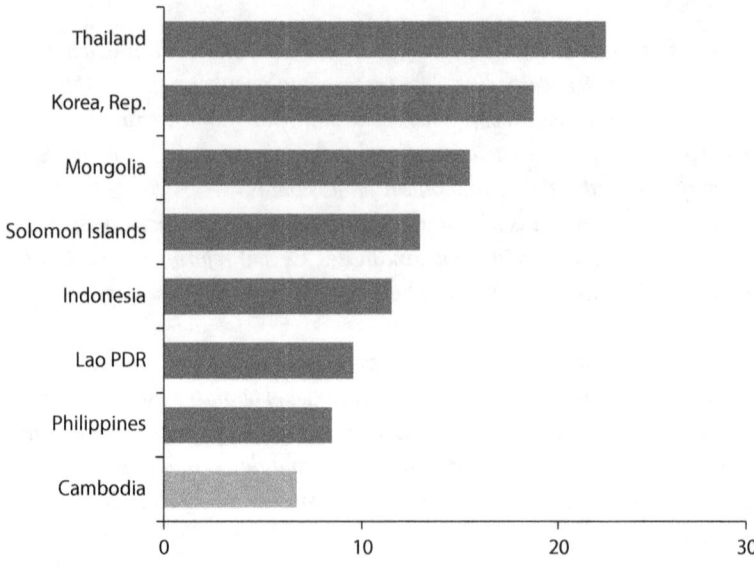

Figure 1.1 Spending per Primary School Student in Southeast Asia and Pacific (Average, 2005–12)
Percentage of GDP per capita

Source: World Bank 2012a.
Note: GDP = gross domestic product.

As in many countries, teacher salaries and related personnel expenses in Cambodia constitute a large portion of recurrent education expenditure—more than 70 percent in 2010–13 (table 1.1) (UNESCO Institute of Statistics 2006; MoEYS 2010). Yet the minimum salary of primary and secondary school teachers as a percentage of GDP is still very low.

Although the government has prioritized education investment to help initiate and sustain more inclusive growth, public education spending has accounted for only about 12.4 percent of recent government budgets, less than in many East Asian and Pacific countries (figure 1.2) (World Bank 2012a). This is confirmed by a recent International Monetary Fund staff report (IMF 2012). Recurrent

Table 1.1 Wage and Other Costs in Recurrent Funding

Variable	2010	2011	2012	2013
Recurrent education expenditure (riel)	824,879	950,185	1,046,419	1,165,415
Personnel cost (% of recurrent)	**73.9**	**72.3**	**72.3**	**72.3**
Nonpersonnel cost (% of recurrent)	26.1	27.7	27.7	27.7

Source: MoEYS 2010.
Note: Boldfaced text indicates the extent of the costs attributable to recurrent expenditures.

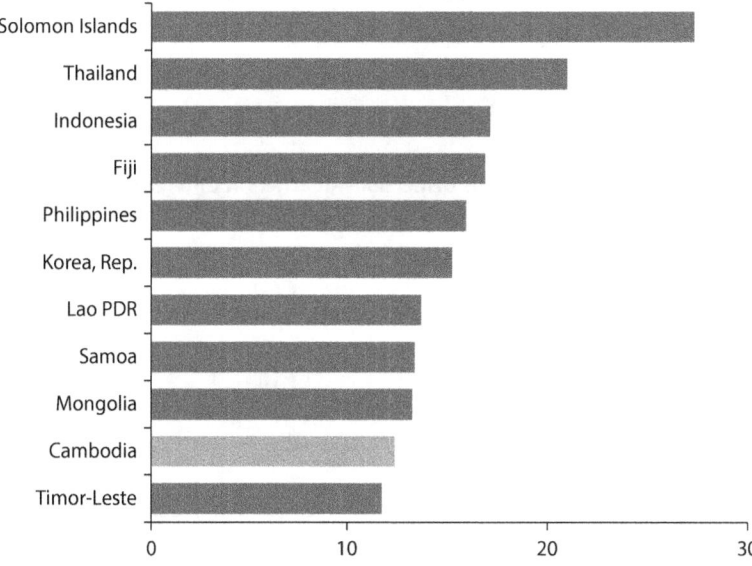

Figure 1.2 Public Spending on Education in East Asia and Pacific (Average, 2007–12)
Percentage of government expenditure

Source: World Bank 2012a.

education expenditure reached 19.2 percent of the national budget in 2007 but only about 16 percent in 2012. Sector allocations have also not been fully spent, due to poor budget planning. In 2010 the education budget was underspent by about $30 million—about 15 percent (figure 1.3).

There is little in-depth analysis of teacher remuneration in Cambodia; perhaps the only well-known fact is that teachers are paid differently at different levels (figure 1.4). Teachers at higher levels earn higher wages. Teachers working in early childhood centers and primary, secondary, and vocational schools earn lower median incomes than teachers in higher education and other education professionals. The earnings dispersion is slightly wider for primary school and early childhood teachers, the group with the lowest reported hourly income. Vocational education teachers experience less variation in hourly income. Other teaching professionals—such as principals and

Figure 1.3 Budgeted and Actual Recurrent Expenditures

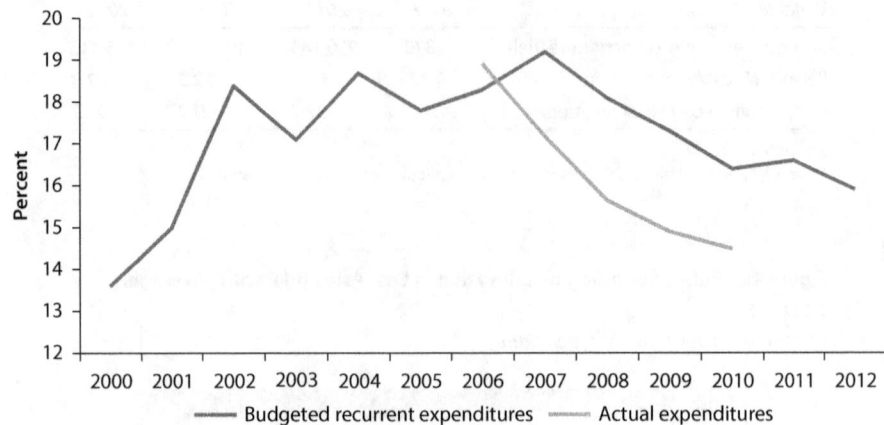

Source: Ministry of Education, Youth, and Sport 2012.

Figure 1.4 Hourly Wage and Its Dispersion—Teachers at Different Levels, 2007–11

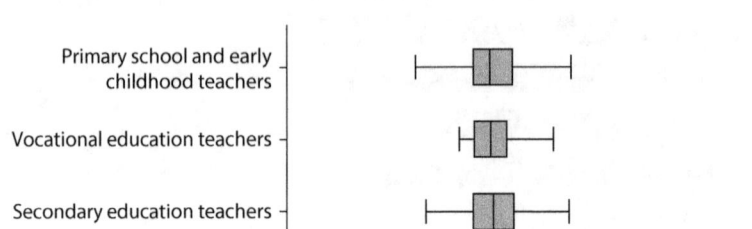

Source: National Institute of Statistics 2007–11.

administrators—and higher education teachers have larger median incomes and larger income variation. Such income differences among education workers may stem from differences in experience, educational attainment, and other characteristics.

Given the dearth of information on teacher salaries and the magnitude of spending on them, a rigorous examination of teacher compensation within the wider Cambodian labor market is much needed. Comparisons with neighboring countries can also help determine whether teacher salaries are regionally competitive.

A Comparative Analysis of Teacher Salaries

Teachers earn less than other professionals in Cambodia, particularly in Phnom Penh (figure 1.5; appendix C.4). Average monthly teacher income (base salary plus monetary incentives) in Phnom Penh is less than 600,000 Cambodian riel, compared with about 750,000 riel for other professionals. These monthly differences are less pronounced in rural areas outside Phnom Penh, perhaps because of recent government policies granting allowances for working in remote locations. But in all locations, teachers on average earn less than other professionals. The average monthly income of both teachers and other professionals falls appreciably outside the capital city.

Teachers earn less than health professionals with similar qualifications (figure 1.6). The median incomes of medical doctors and other health professionals, for instance, are higher than those of university teachers and other education professionals, respectively. Health professionals, particularly nurses, midwives, and medical doctors, also exhibit wider wage dispersion among themselves than teachers do. Teachers may thus not have adequate motivation to aspire to higher levels of the profession.

Teacher salaries have increased recently, but not quickly enough to close the gap with other professionals. From 2007 to 2011, the average monthly nominal wage increased by about 144,000 riel (table 1.2). During this period, other professionals continued to earn higher wages than teachers, so the earnings gap has not changed much.

Other professionals also are paid better with respect to the minimum wage. Cambodian law guarantees a minimum wage but does not specify a standard amount. Instead, minimum wages vary across industries and regions. The garment and shoe industry has a specific minimum wage, which increased from $40 to $50 a month in October 2011 (IMF 2012; UNESCAP 2012). The ratio

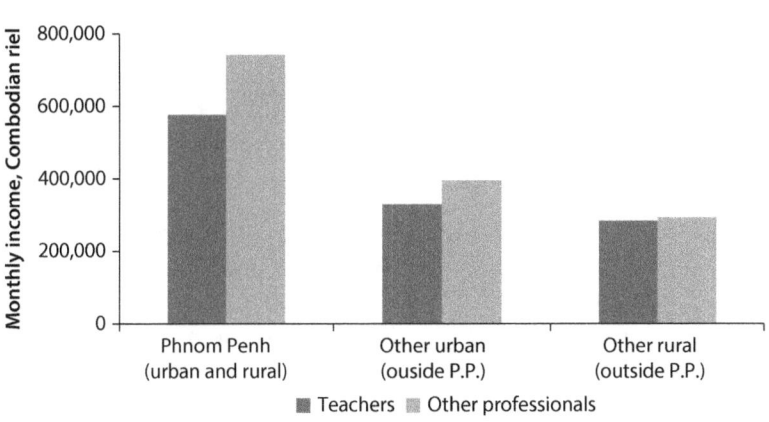

Figure 1.5 Average Monthly Wage Income of Teachers and Other Professionals, 2007–11, by Region

Source: National Institute of Statistics 2007–11.
Note: P.P. = Phnom Penh.

Figure 1.6 Hourly Wage and Its Dispersion—Teachers versus Health Professionals, 2007–11

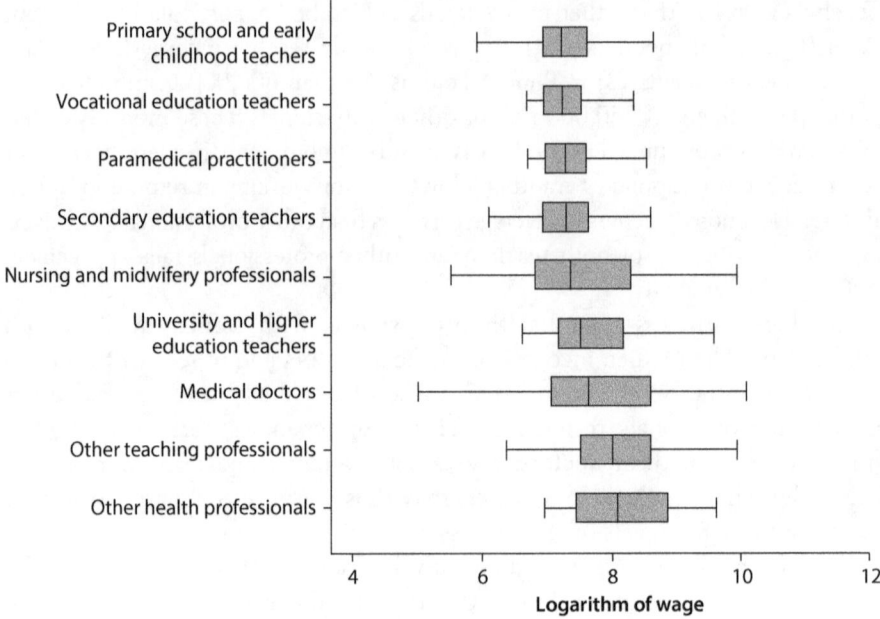

Source: National Institute of Statistics 2007–11.

Table 1.2 Average Monthly Nominal Income of Teachers and Other Professionals versus Minimum Wage in Garment Sector, and Income Growth Rate, 2007–11

	Monthly income (riel)		Yearly growth rate (%)		Average wage per minimum wage in the garment sector (riel)	
Year	Teachers	Other professionals	Teachers	Other professionals	Teachers	Other professionals
2007	304,538	564,552			1.5	2.8
2008	345,917	617,808	13.6	9.4	1.7	3.0
2009	345,217	575,645	−0.2	−6.8	1.7	2.8
2010	424,125	739,223	22.9	28.4	2.0	3.5
2011	448,035	746,768	5.6	1.0	2.2	3.7

Sources: World Bank 2012b; National Institute of Statistics 2007–11.

of average teacher income to this minimum wage increased from 1.5 in 2007 to 2.2 in 2011 (see table 1.2). Other professionals did better during this period.

Similar gaps appear when comparing wages and the poverty line.[1] A typical teacher earns about three times the earning cutoff for the poverty line. Household size is not accounted for, so a typical teacher with more than three dependents would fall below the poverty line. But other professionals earn about five times the poverty line income (table 1.3).

International Comparisons

We compared incomes of teachers and other professionals in Cambodia with those in Thailand and Vietnam (table 1.4; appendix tables C.4 and C.5). Thailand is the only country of the three where teachers earn a higher average monthly income than do professionals in other industries. In both Cambodia and Vietnam teachers earn less than other professionals. But the relative income of teachers is much lower in Cambodia.

Due to differences in purchasing power of the U.S. dollar in these countries, we refrain from directly comparing monthly incomes. Instead, we calculate the percentage of teachers' average monthly income relative to that of other professionals (figure 1.7). Teachers in Cambodia earned about 60 percent of the average monthly income of other Cambodian professionals in 2011. In Vietnam, they earned 88 percent and in Thailand 144 percent. During 2007–11, teachers in Cambodia earned about 54–60 percent of the monthly income of other professionals, in Vietnam 88–98 percent, and in Thailand 138–49 percent.

Table 1.3 Daily Income of Teachers and Other Professionals versus Poverty Line, 2007–11
Riel

	Teachers			Other professionals		
Year	Average income	Poverty line	Average income/ poverty line	Average income	Poverty line	Average income/ poverty line
2007	10,151	3,493	2.9	19,172	3,493	5.5
2008	11,531	4,895	2.4	20,731	4,895	4.2
2009	11,507	4,095	2.8	19,381	4,095	4.7
2010	14,138	4,510	3.1	24,822	4,510	5.5
2011	14,934	4,842	3.1	24,990	4,842	5.2

Source: National Institute of Statistics 2007–11.

Table 1.4 Average Nominal Income of Teachers and Other Professionals in Cambodia, Thailand, and Vietnam
Dollars per month

	Cambodia		Thailand		Vietnam	
Year	Teachers	Other professionals	Teachers	Other professionals	Teachers	Other professionals
2007	75	139	485	340	—	—
2008	85	152	542	364	—	—
2009	83	139	518	358	148	151
2010	101	177	565	408	151	171
2011	110	184	632	440	167	190

Sources: World Bank 2012b; Ministry of Planning and Investment 2012 (Vietnam); Ministry of Information and Communication Technology 2011 (Thailand); National Institute of Statistics 2007–11 (Cambodia).
Note: — = not available.

Figure 1.7 Monthly Income of Teachers as a Percentage of Monthly Income of Other Professionals, Cambodia, Vietnam, and Thailand, 2007–11
Percent

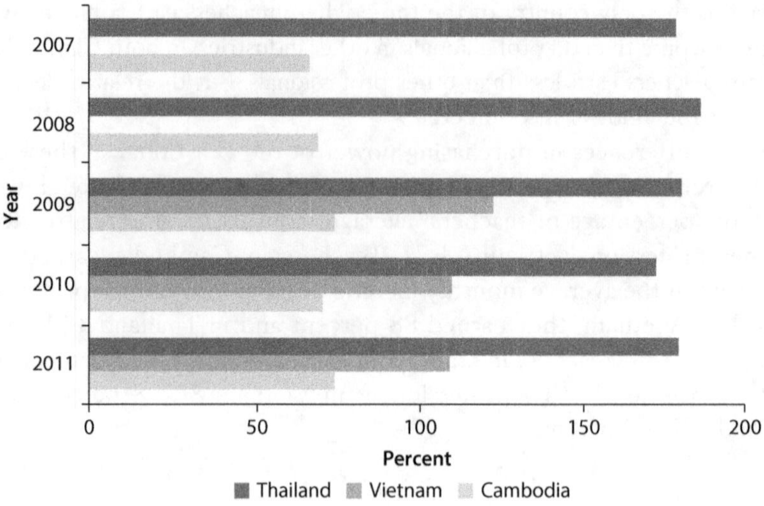

Source: Calculations, using World Bank 2012b; Ministry of Planning and Investment 2012 (Vietnam); Ministry of Information and Communication Technology 2011 (Thailand); National Institute of Statistics 2007–11 (Cambodia).

Unpacking Earning Differences

Teachers' average earnings are consistently lower than those of other professionals nationally and regionally. But these income differences do not necessarily imply labor market disadvantage. The disparities could be driven by differences in human capital endowments, such as years of education or professional qualifications. To distinguish between pay disadvantage and the effects of endowment differences, we employed Oaxaca-Blinder decomposition analysis (appendix B).

First, we explore the mean and standard deviation of variables that could capture the differences in human resource endowments and earnings (table 1.5). During 2007–11, teachers consistently earned lower wages per hour, except in 2011. They also worked fewer hours per month—196 hours, compared with 213 hours by other professionals. There was no significant difference in hours worked among teachers and other professionals with secondary education or above—teachers worked 190 hours, other professionals 185 hours. Other professionals had an average of one more year of education than teachers, and a larger proportion of them had lower secondary education certification or above—as well as a bachelor's degree or above. Teachers and other professionals thus exhibit clear differences in endowments and earnings.

During 2008–11, teachers' wages exhibited high compression (figure 1.8). In all years, the distribution of teacher salaries tends to be more concentrated around the mean than that of other professionals, in line with the lower standard

Table 1.5 Mean and Standard Deviation of Selected Variables for Teachers and Other Professionals, 2007–11

Variable	2007 Teachers	2007 Other professionals	2008 Teachers	2008 Other professionals	2009 Teachers	2009 Other professionals	2010 Teachers	2010 Other professionals	2011 Teachers	2011 Other professionals
Hourly earnings	1.74	3.01	2.02	3.33	2.03	3.11	1.76	2.08	2.23	2.16
(thousands of riel)	(2.55)	(7.70)	(2.35)	(5.53)	(1.97)	(4.06)	(1.21)	(3.46)	(2.84)	(2.32)
Hours worked per month	181	193	179	191	185	194	217	247	219	239
	(54)	(52)	(53)	(50)	(59)	(58)	(70)	(70)	(58)	(57)
Monthly income	305	575	337	621	337	581	424	739	448	747
(thousands of riel)	(495)	(1,457)	(354)	(1,029)	(311)	(803)	(510)	(843)	(565)	(698)
Years of education	11.7	11.0	11.8	11.4	11.8	10.6	12.4	11.1	12.7	11.9
	(3.7)	(4.4)	(3.1)	(4.5)	(3.1)	(4.5)	(3.3)	(4.6)	(2.8)	(4.23)
Lower education certificate and above (%)	58	40	40	38	48	33	65	45	71	53
	(49)	(49)	(49)	(49)	(50)	(47)	(48)	(50)	(46)	(50)
Bachelor's degree and above (%)	16	25	7	26	12	20	17	26	14	32
	(37)	(43)	(25)	(44)	(32)	(40)	(38)	(44)	(35)	(47)
Female (%)	47	33	48	31	45	29	41	31	50	33
	(50)	(47)	(50)	(46)	(50)	(46)	(49)	(46)	(50)	(47)
Number of observation	137	907	121	898–1,019	398	678–1,392	66–121	109–794	60–121	111–823

Source: National Institute of Statistics 2007–11.
Note: Values in parentheses are standard deviations of the respective variables.

Figure 1.8 Hourly Wage Distribution for Teachers and Other Professionals, 2011

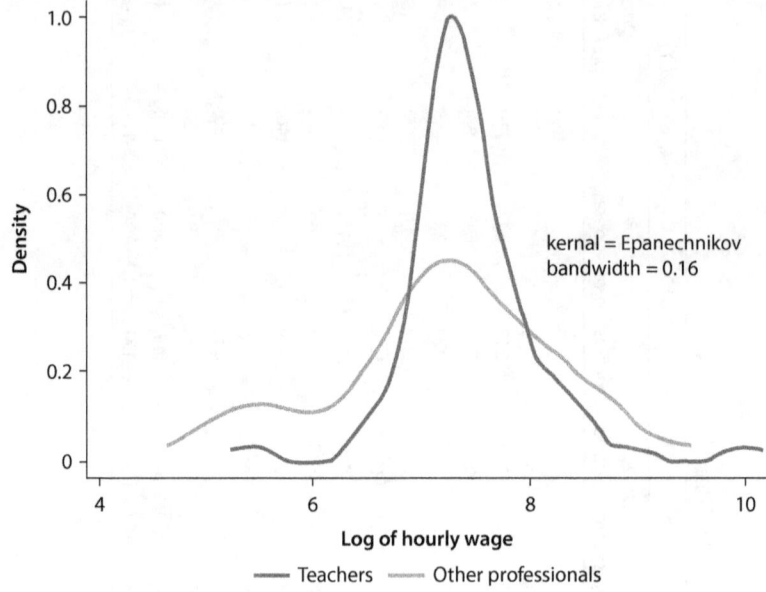

Source: Calculations from National Institute of Statistics 2008–11.

deviation in the hourly teacher income reported in table 1.2. The median hourly teacher income appeared to be lower than for other professionals in 2008 and 2009, but the gap narrowed in 2010 and 2011. Gaining a teaching position guarantees a salary within a fairly narrow band, with little risk of a much lower wage than other teachers, but also little chance of a higher one.

There Is a Significant Wage Disadvantage for Teachers, Particularly Female Teachers

We used pooled cross-section data from the Cambodia Socio-Economic Survey (National Institute of Statistics 2007–11) to analyze monthly income differences between teachers and other professionals in Cambodia (table 1.6; appendix table C.2). The overall difference in the logarithm of monthly income is 0.33, of which 0.09 is the result of the endowment difference; 0.16 is due to the coefficient difference; and the remaining 0.07 is the result of the interaction of differences in coefficients and endowments.

To establish whether teachers are systematically disadvantaged in the labor market, we conducted a twofold decomposition by estimating equation B.8 (appendix B). The results suggest that half of the difference in monthly income of teachers and other professionals (0.168) is the result of endowment differences, while the other half (0.166) is the result of pay disadvantage (see table 1.6). To facilitate interpretation, we transform the

Table 1.6 Oaxaca-Blinder Decomposition of Income of Teachers and Other Professionals (Dependent Variable: Logarithm of Monthly Income)

Overall	Threefold decomposition (equation B.7)		Twofold decomposition (equation B.8)	
	Coefficient	z	Coefficient	z
Group 1: Other professionals	12.90	856.42***	12.90	856.42***
Group 2: Teachers	12.57	621.67***	12.57	621.67***
Differences	**0.33**	**13.22*** **	**0.33**	**13.22*** **
Endowments	0.09	3.51***		
Coefficients	0.16	5.69***		
Interaction	0.07	2.35*		
"Explained"			0.168	8.30***
"Unexplained"			0.166	5.93***

Source: National Institute of Statistics 2007–11.
Note: The included explanatory variables, not shown in this table, are education, qualification certificates and degree, potential experience, urban and Phnom Penh dummies, gender, and marital status.
Significance level: * = 10 percent; *** = 1 percent.

Oaxaca-Blinder decomposition output from logarithm to level. Accordingly, the monthly income gap is 113,354 riel, with the mean monthly income of other professionals and teachers being 399,949 and 286,594 riel, respectively. This translates into a 39.6 percent pay gap between teachers and other professionals. But endowment differences only partially explain this gap. About 56,677 riel per month, translating into a yearly amount of 18 percent of an average Cambodian's annual income, is not explained by such endowment differences. We cannot identify any other unobserved variables that may drive this result.

Female teachers also earn less than their male colleagues (appendix table C.2). As discussed, such income differences cannot be interpreted as the result of labor market disadvantage without analyzing human capital endowments. Accordingly, we apply Oaxaca-Blinder decomposition for mean wage differences between female and male teachers (appendix table C.3), resulting in a difference in mean monthly incomes (in logarithmic terms) of 0.165. This translates into a 46,893 riel (equivalent to 17.9 percent) difference in mean monthly incomes between male and female teachers, who respectively earn an average of 309,043 and 262,150 riel. Only 33 percent of this wage gap between female and male teachers is explained by human capital endowment differences; the remaining 66 percent, by pay disadvantage.

Between 2011 and 2013 (figure 1.9), the mean monthly basic salary of teachers and education professionals grew, but other benefits, such as the pedagogical allowance and functional salary allowance, have not changed substantially. To determine how much these new developments have bridged the gap between teachers and other professionals requires a follow-up evaluation as new Cambodia Socio-Economic Survey data become available.

Figure 1.9 Recent Improvements in Average Monthly Teacher Income by Level, 2011–13

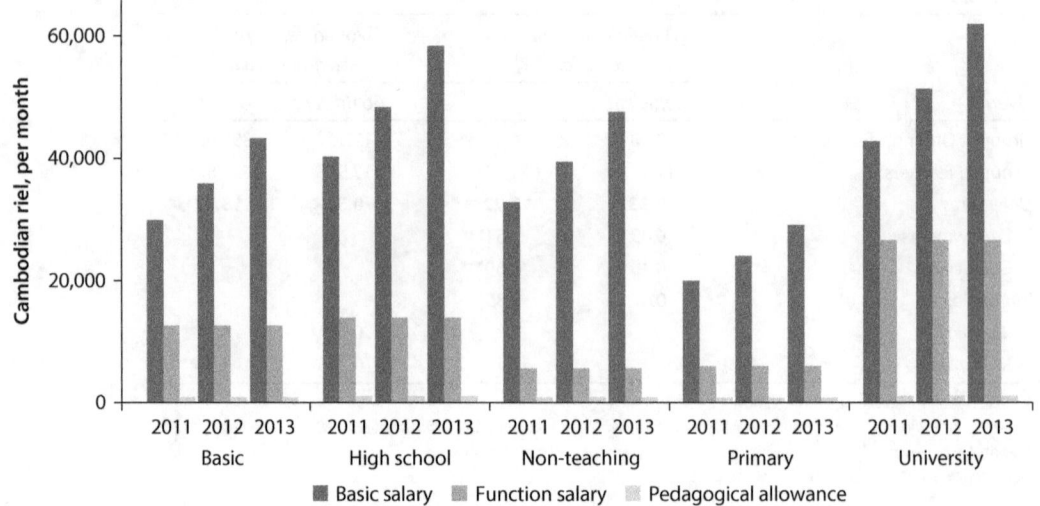

Source: National Institute of Statistics 2007–11; Ministry of Education, Youth, and Sport 2012.

What Teachers Say about Salaries

In the 2012 teacher policy survey of 150 primary schools (see chapter 4), almost all teachers (92 percent) indicated they were aware of recent teacher salary increases, but only about 40 percent felt that the salary increase had made their professional and personal lives easier. Almost all indicated that this was due to the extra money helping to pay bills and support themselves (and their families) and was not due to an improved work environment or working less in a secondary job.

Teachers report a monthly base salary average of about 335,000 riel, or $82 (table 1.7), more than double the average reported by teachers in the 2007 Public Expenditure Tracking Survey.[2] Urban teachers report the highest base salaries (about 350,000), followed by rural (328,000) and remote (265,000) teachers. The gap between urban and remote teachers is thus about 85,000 riel a month ($21.25), about 25 percent of the average teacher's salary. When computing hourly wages (by dividing the monthly salary by the monthly hours worked [weekly multiplied by four]), we confirm that urban teachers have the highest hourly pay (4,275 riel), much higher than the remote school teacher average (2,608 riel). This difference is driven by higher pay in urban schools and longer hours in remote ones.

Consistent with the evidence from the Cambodia Socio-Economic Surveys, teacher salaries vary across and within spatial categories, based on the standard deviations computed in table 1.7. But they do not vary much based on individual performance reviews and productivity. The results of regressions for teacher monthly pay and hourly wage based on reported hours provide some clues about teacher pay dynamics, including equity and pay distribution (table 1.8).

As expected, primary school teachers with more experience and education earn more money. Males have higher salaries than females, and teachers with certification have higher salaries than noncertified teachers (a small group). Contract teachers receive much lower pay. Not surprisingly, larger workloads, such as double shift teaching and teaching multiple grades, give lower hourly pay. So incentives for these teaching arrangements—which increase total pay—do not make them equal to others in hourly compensation. Teachers in remote schools, even when controlling for experience and other factors, also receive lower hourly wages.

Table 1.7 Teacher Salaries, Monthly and Hourly Average
Riel

Category	Total monthly salary	Hourly average
All teachers	334,971	3,778
	(77,775)	(1,228)
Urban	**350,199***	**4,275***
	(62,115)	(1,032)
Rural	**327,803***	**3,451***
	(78,552)	(1,205)
Remote	**264,984***	**2,608***
	(81,905)	(1,261)

Source: World Bank 2012b.
Note: Standard deviations in parentheses. Results are based on weighted data. Boldfaced text emphasizes the distinctions between categories.
* = Category mean is significantly different from average at 0.05 level.

Table 1.8 Covariates of Teacher Total Salary and Hourly Average

Variable	Total salary	Wage
Teacher is male	0.04***	0.06***
	(2.74)	(3.49)
Teacher years of education	0.007**	0.008
	(1.94)	(1.43)
Teacher experience	0.02***	0.02***
	(11.03)	(8.45)
Teacher experience—this school	0.001	0.001
	(0.48)	(0.36)
Teacher has double shift bonus	−0.07	−0.37***
	(−0.66)	(−4.46)
Teacher has remote school bonus	−0.03	−0.01
	(−1.53)	(−0.28)
Number of grades taught	0.07	−0.21**
	(0.87)	(−2.24)

table continues next page

Table 1.8 Covariates of Teacher Total Salary and Hourly Average *(continued)*

Variable	Total salary	Wage
Type of teacher		
Head teacher	0.03	0.03
	(1.34)	(1.34)
Contract teacher	–0.22**	–0.22**
	(–2.55)	(–2.55)
School size	0.001	0.001
	(0.01)	(0.79)
School is rural	0.02	–0.02
	(1.19)	(–0.71)
School is remote	–0.05	–0.13**
	(–1.34)	(–1.98)
Parents % with cell phone	–0.08*	–0.08**
	(–1.99)	(–1.99)
Parents average education	0.01**	0.01**
	(2.52)	(2.52)
Sample size (number)	577	577
Explained variance (R^2)	0.51	0.70

Sources: World Bank 2012b; various databases.
Note: Dependent variables are measured in natural log. Results are based on weighted data. Not all variable coefficients are presented, complete results available upon request.
Significance level: * = 0.10, ** = 0.05, *** = 0.01.

Payment Delays

Underpayment, facilitation fees, and delayed salary payments are major sources of discontent among teachers (table 1.9) (Benveniste, Marshall, and Aranjo 2008). Alarmingly, only about 37 percent of teachers report that they "always" receive the full amount of their salaries, and between 43 and 51 percent report that they "never" do. Facilitation fees are common in rural and remote areas, though on average they only amount to about 3,800 riel ($0.95).

Almost all teachers report delays in receiving their salaries. The average delay length, about 10 days, varies little by school location. In remote schools, 10 percent of primary school teachers indicated that they "sometimes" miss school to collect pay, and 5.7 percent noted that they "always" miss class for this.

Trainee Salary Expectations

In the 2012 Teacher Training Center (TTC) Survey of 10 TTCs (see chapter 2), students preparing to become lower secondary teachers (regional teaching training center [RTTC] trainees) said they expect to earn 345,000 riel a month (about 85 dollars), more than students preparing to become primary teachers (provincial teaching training center [PTTC] trainees) (242,000 riel a month, or about 60 dollars).[3] The lowest reported expected salaries are among 9+2 program and remote school trainees (table 1.10). Trainees do not feel positive about their expected salaries. About 80 percent feel that their salaries will be lower or much lower than those in other professions. They also do not consider entry into a TTC very difficult.

Table 1.9 Teacher Payment Problems
Percent, unless otherwise indicated

Variable	All teachers	By location		
		Urban	Rural	Remote
How often are you paid the full amount of your salary?				
Always	36.8	36.5	37.1	36.9
Usually	9.6	7.2	11.0	16.7
Seldom	4.0	4.5	3.7	2.8
Never	49.7	51.8	48.3	43.7
Do you pay a "facilitation fee"?	26.7	**19.4+**	31.7	43.1
If yes, how much? (riel)	3,828	3,357	4,193	2,899
Have you had any delays in basic salary payment? (Yes)	77.2	81.7	73.0	83.1
If yes, how many days?	10.2	10.5	9.8	12.5
Do you ever miss school to collect pay?				
Never	92.4	92.8	92.6	84.3
Sometimes	5.1	5.1	4.9	10.0
Always	2.5	2.1	2.5	5.7
Sample size (number)	677	138	478	52

Source: World Bank 2012b.
Note: Results are based on weighted data.
+ = Category mean is significantly different from average at 0.10 level.

Table 1.10 TTC Trainee Salary Expectations and Difficulty of Entering TTC
Percent, unless otherwise indicated

Variable	Full samples		PTTC subsamples		
	RTTC	PTTC	12+2	9+2	Remote
Expected salary (thousands of riel)	345	**242***	281	**199***	**201***
How salary compares with other professions					
Much lower	20.6	19.1	22.1	14.6	14.6
Lower	57.1	67.7	67.6	67.9	70.0
About the same	11.3	10.4	7.5	15.0	14.6
Higher	11.0	2.7	2.9	2.5	0.8
How difficult is entry into TTC?					
Very difficult	35.9	19.0	20.8	16.3	15.1
Difficult	54.8	71.2	71.9	70.2	72.5
Not difficult	8.3	8.1	6.2	10.9	9.7
Easy	1.0	1.7	1.1	2.6	2.7
Sample size (number)	301	651	387	264	257

Source: World Bank 2012c.
Note: PTTC = provincial teaching training centers; RTTC = regional teaching training center; TTC = teacher training center. All results are based on weighted data. Tests of significance are used to compare RTTC and PTTC averages (significant differences highlighted in PTTC column), 12+2 and 9+2 averages (significant differences highlighted in 9+2 column), and remote and nonremote PTTC averages (highlighted in remote column).
* = Difference in average/percentage is significantly different at 0.05 level (two-tail).
+ = Difference in average/percentage is significantly different at 0.10 level. Boldface also used to highlight significant differences.

TTC Selectivity

Given the professions' relatively low wages, it is perhaps not surprising that teaching does not attract Cambodia's top graduates. Very few of those pursuing teaching as a career are top scorers on the grade 12 exit exam. None of those enrolled in TTCs scored in the A or B range; the majority of TTC enrollees scored in the D and E range. The scale according to the Department of General Secondary Education is: A=Excellence, B=Very Good, C=Good, D=Satisfactory, E=Limited Achievement, F=Fail, with an intended even distribution across categories (figure 1.10).

The caliber of students applying to TTCs is lower than those of other postsecondary applicants because of low TTC admissions requirements. As of 2012, most other fields in Cambodia required at least a D on the grade 12 leaving exam to apply to their courses and take the entrance exam. The high number of TTC applicants scoring E are not even eligible to apply to these other courses, making TTCs "attractive" to individuals with few other options. The TTC entrance exam date is later than that for virtually all other major postsecondary fields in Cambodia—after other entrance exam results are known. Thus, those who fail the entrance exams of major universities often take the TTC exam as a back-up plan. The nearly 40 percent of TTC enrollees with a self-reported E had few other courses to apply to.

Each TTC receives more than 1,200 applications a year but accepts only about 160, an acceptance rate of only 15.6 percent (weighted). Although demand is higher than supply, more than one-third of TTCs report difficulties in

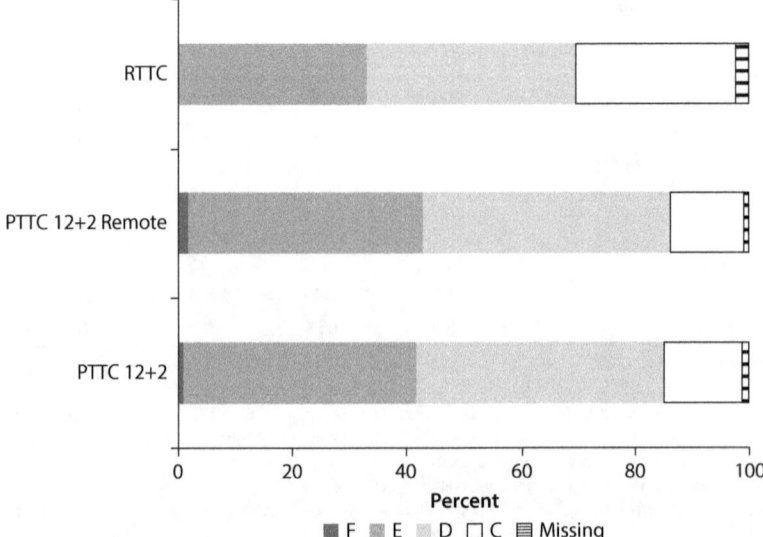

Figure 1.10 Trainee Self-Reported Grade 12 Exam Result, 12+2 Samples Only

Source: World Bank 2012c.
Note: PTTC = provincial teaching training center; RTTC = regional teaching training center.

recruiting qualified candidates and dissatisfaction with enrollee caliber. This issue was much more pronounced among PTTCs, suggesting a perceived link between applicant quality and teaching level. When TTC directors and personnel were asked how to improve the qualifications of candidates, their open-ended responses suggested reforming and removing any unfair and informal practices from the entrance examination process.

Entering Teaching

Trainees indicated that they chose teaching as a profession because of its importance, job security, and respectability, and because they like it (figure 1.11). They feel positive about the work and the workplace environment. But they perceive teaching to be noncompetitive in terms of pay and job difficulty (figure 1.12).

Trainers agree (figure 1.13), saying that teaching compares favorably with other professions in job security, holiday time, the amount of training required, and work load and conditions, but less favorably in promotion chances and salaries.

Teachers report satisfaction with their work conditions and school support systems. Widely attended technical meetings encourage teacher–teacher interaction, but teachers also express the need for a more dynamic and collaborative training environment (see chapter 4).

According to year 2 trainees, acceptance into a TTC and getting a job after graduation are the easiest aspects of teaching (figure 1.14). The hardest aspects are completing the training and getting job security.

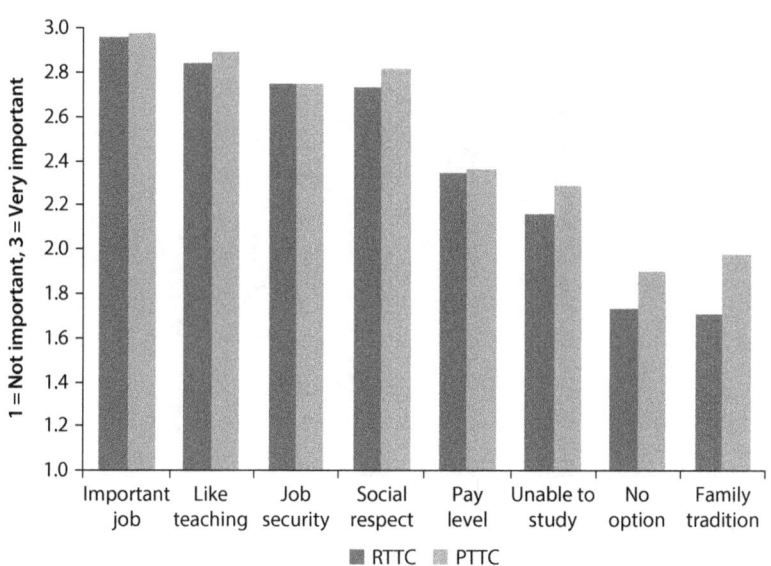

Figure 1.11 Reasons for Entering Teaching, by RTTC-PTTC

Source: World Bank 2012c.
Note: PTTC = provincial teaching training center; RTTC = regional teaching training center.

Figure 1.12 Trainee Comparisons of Teaching with Other Professions

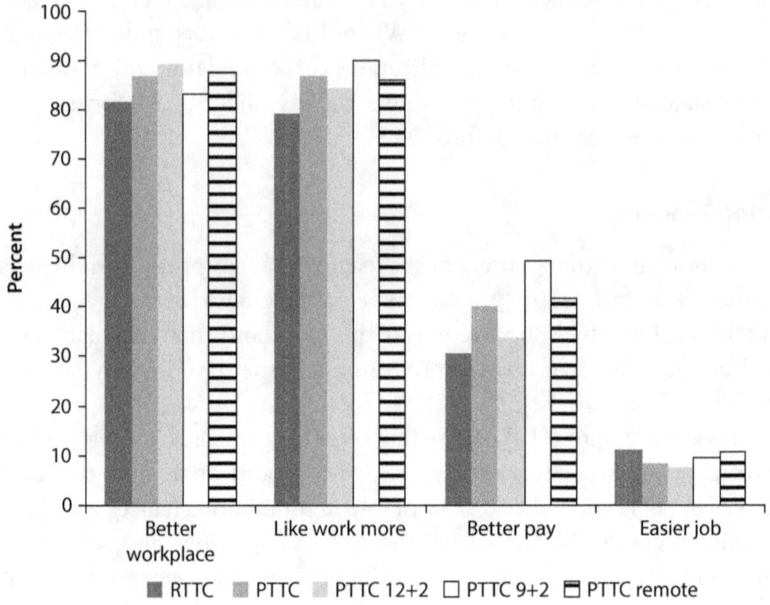

Source: World Bank 2012c.
Note: PTTC = provincial teaching training center; RTTC = regional teaching training center.

Figure 1.13 Trainer Comparisons of Teaching with Other Professions

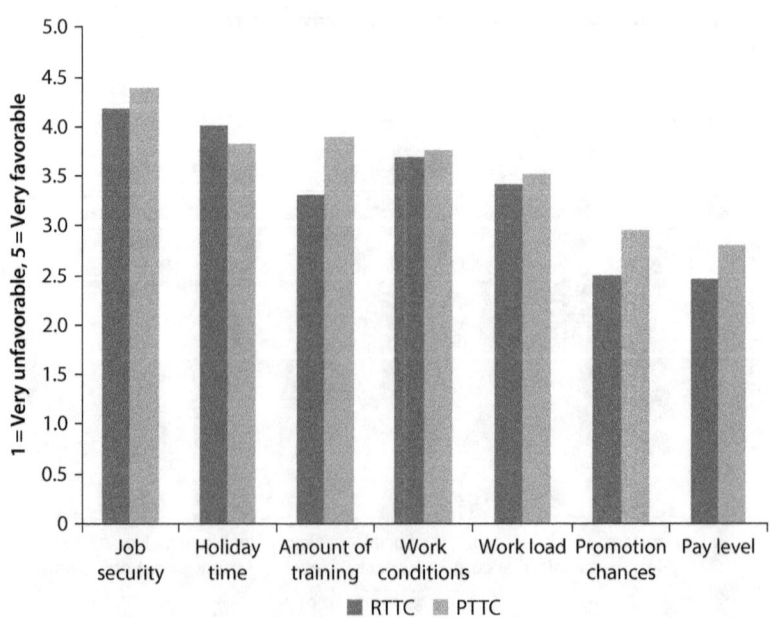

Source: World Bank 2012c.
Note: PTTC = provincial teaching training center; RTTC = regional teaching training center.

Figure 1.14 Trainee Ranking of Easiest Aspects of Teaching, RTTC-PTTC Samples

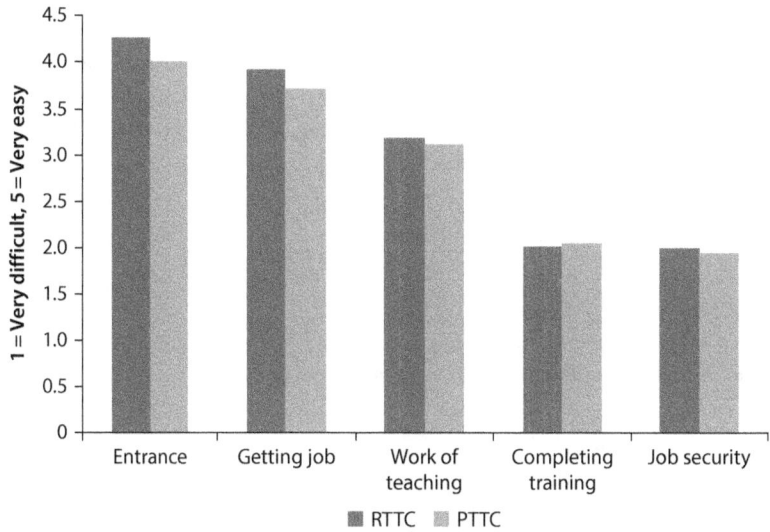

Source: World Bank 2012c.
Note: PTTC = provincial teaching training center; RTTC = regional teaching training center.

Notes

1. The poverty line varies regionally. In this table, we provide an average of the poverty line, weighted by the proportion of samples from different regions. This explains a slight variation over time, particularly the decline in value in 2009 and 2010.
2. All of the teacher salary and hours worked data are self-reported in this section. These data are compared with data from the Cambodia Socio-Economic Surveys later in this study.
3. RTTCs are regional teaching training centers and PTTCs are provincial teaching training centers. Upper secondary school graduates are known as 12+2 graduates and lower secondary school graduates as 9+2 graduates.

Bibliography

Benveniste, Luis, Jeffery Marshall, and M. Caridad Aranjo. 2008. *Teaching in Cambodia*. Washington, DC: World Bank.

Bloom, Richard, James A. Dunn, and William C. Morse. 1964. "Data-Source Consensus: A Fundamental Problem in Classroom Research." *Journal of Educational Measurement* 1 (2): 119–23.

Cambodia Administrative Reform General Secretariat. 2010. Human Resource Management Information System (database). Government of Cambodia, Phnom Penh.

Education Management Information System (database). Various years. Ministry of Education, Youth, and Sports. Government of Cambodia, Phnom Penh.

Filmer, Deon, and Norbert Schady. 2009. "School Enrollment, Selection, and Test Scores." Policy Research Working Paper 4998, World Bank, Washington, DC.

Hanushek, Eric A., and Ludger Woessmannn. 2007. "The Role of Education Quality in Economic Growth." Policy Research Working Paper 4122, World Bank, Washington, DC.

———. 2008. "The Role of Cognitive Skills in Economic Development." *Journal of Economic Literature* 46 (3): 607–88.

Hanushek, Eric A., and Steven G. Rivkin. 2010. "Generalizations about Using Value-Added Measures of Teacher Quality." *American Economic Review* 100 (2): 267–71.

IMF (International Monetary Fund). 2012. *Cambodia: 2011 Article IV Consultation*. Country Report 12/46, IMF, Washington, DC.

Ministry of Education, Youth, and Sports. 2010 and 2014. "Education Master Plan." Government of Cambodia, Phnon Penh.

Ministry of Information and Communication Technology. Various years. *The Labor Force Survey*. Bangkok: National Statistical Office, Thailand.

Ministry of Planning and Investment. Various years. *The Labor Force Survey*. Hanoi: General Statistics Office, Vietnam.

National Institute of Statistics. Various years. *Cambodia Socio-Economic Survey*. Phnom Penh: Royal Government of Cambodia, Ministry of Planning.

Psacharopoulos, George, and Anthony H. Patrinos. 2002. "Returns to Investment in Education: A Further Update." Policy Research Working Paper 2881, World Bank, Washington, DC.

Stallings, Jane A., and David H. Kaskowitz. 1974. *Follow Through Classroom Observation Evaluation 1972–1973*. SRI Project URU-7370. Menlo Park, CA: Stanford Research Institute.

Theodore W. Schultz. 1961. "Investment in Human Capital." *The American Economic Review* 51 (1): 1–17.

UNESCAP (United Nations Economic and Social Commission for Asia and Pacific). 2012. *Traders Manual for Least Developed Countries: Cambodia*. New York: United Nations.

UNESCO (United Nations Educational, Scientific and Cultural Organization) Institute for Statistics. 2006. *Teachers and Educational Quality: Monitoring Global Needs for 2015*. Montreal, QC: UNESCO.

World Bank. 2009. *Education at a Glance: Cambodia*. Washington, DC: World Bank.

———. 2012a. *World Development Indicators 2012*. Washington, DC: World Bank.

———. 2012b. "Teacher Survey." World Bank, Washington, DC.

———. 2012c. "Teacher Training College Survey." World Bank, Washington, DC.

CHAPTER 2

How Well Does the Cambodian Teacher Training System Train Teachers?

Key Messages

Despite adequate facilities and positive perceptions of school environments, the majority of Cambodia's teacher trainers fail to provide sufficient content mastery and student-centered pedagogy.

Teacher standards have not been integrated into teacher training center (TTC) instruction, undermining their utility. Though required, in practice teacher standards are not a part of the curriculum in half of schools. Many teacher trainers have not heard of the teacher standards, and even trainers with written copies seldom incorporate them into their classes. There is a major disconnect among the Ministry of Education, Youth, and Sports (MoEYS) teacher training goals, the stated curricular guidelines, and what is happening in TTC classrooms.

Teacher trainers work in an environment with little contact, support, or collaboration. This isolation, especially without well-defined mechanisms to assess training effectiveness (such as visits from the Provincial Office of Education), reduces opportunities to raise quality.

The teaching and learning environment in the average TTC is teacher centered and far from interactive. Dictating lessons with little feedback or applied activities or having students copy off the board for extended periods, suggests low-quality instruction. In only about one-third of the classrooms did teacher trainees ask the trainers questions.

Effective Teacher Education

Preparing teachers with useful training and experience is critical to achieving high performance in the classroom. Top-performing school systems (for example, in Finland and the Republic of Korea) recruit teachers in the higher echelons of

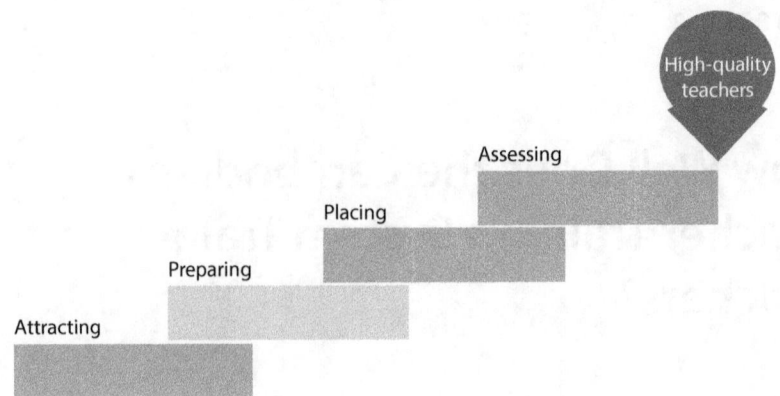

their academic cohorts, as measured by test scores and grade point averages, and equip these recruits with effective teaching experience and exceptional classroom skills.

Effective teacher education programs can improve student learning substantially. Teacher preparation contributes more than any other factor to student achievement in reading and mathematics, both before and after controlling for student poverty and socioeconomic status, and teachers' effects on student achievement are additive and cumulative (Darling-Hammond 2000).[1] So preparation and development opportunities have paramount importance for teaching quality and effectiveness.

A 2012 national survey of 10 TTCs, with 1,000 primary and secondary trainees, gathered three sources of information. First, detailed questionnaires for trainees, trainers, and TTC directors asked about trainee study experiences and labor market expectations (discussed in chapter 1). Second, trainees and trainers took a pedagogical content knowledge test and a mathematics test covering content from grades 6 and 9 curricula (discussed in chapter 5). Finally, TTC classrooms were observed using an instrument to assess classroom behavior and time on task.

These three instruments assess the next generation of teaching in Cambodia and offer insight into how well the teacher training system is functioning. They also shed light on several auxiliary questions:

- What are the TTCs' physical and human resource conditions?
- What is the pedagogical model in TTC classrooms?
- How knowledgeable are TTC trainees and trainers in mathematics and pedagogy?

Our analysis indicates that reform is urgently needed. Despite adequate facilities and positive perceptions of school environments, Cambodia's teacher trainers fail to provide sufficient content mastery and student-centered pedagogy.

How the Teacher Training System Functions

In the late 1970s, 75 percent of teachers and 96 percent of university students were killed under the Khmer Rouge. After the fall of the Khmer Rouge in 1979, Cambodians worked quickly to reconstruct the education system by opening schools and recruiting and training a new generation of teachers. One of the earliest teacher training schemes was a short-term course in 1980 for preprimary, primary, and secondary teachers. In 1982, provincial TTCs started to offer more formal, year-long preservice training courses for aspiring primary teachers. In 1990, this training was strengthened and extended to a two-year course. In 1982, a year-long preservice training began at the Royal University of Phnom Penh for both lower and upper secondary school teachers.

TTCs now cover four distinct categories: preschool teacher training center (PSTTC), primary for provincial teacher training center (PTTC), lower secondary for regional teacher training center (RTTC), and upper secondary, conducted by the National Institute of Education (NIE). There are 26 TTCs spread throughout the country (table 2.1). In 2012, some 7,322 trainees were enrolled in year 1 and year 2 programs in all TTCs and the NIE. Courses are free, and students receive a small monthly stipend of 9,000 riel.

The four teacher training categories have slightly different entry requirements. The PSTTCs and PTTCs require two-year courses for upper secondary school graduates (12+2) or, in areas where upper secondary school graduates are hard to find, lower secondary school graduates (9+2).[1] RTTC trainees must have completed at least the upper secondary school sequence (12+2). NIE offers a one-year course to bachelor's degree holders (bachelor's+1) for upper secondary teacher placement.

Entering a TTC requires two examinations and an application. Grades 9 and 12 students take their national leaving examinations in early July; the results are announced in late August. Students interested in entering PSTTCs, PTTCs, and RTTCs submit their applications to Cambodia's Provincial Offices of Education during the last week of July and take a TTC entrance examination in mid-October. The semester starts on the first of November. For second-year trainees, the semester starts on the first of October, similar to the regular academic year.

According to Cambodia's Council for Administrative Reform, 5,000 teacher trainees are accepted each year for all levels from PSTTCs to NIE. Candidate examination scores are ranked and accepted by MoEYS based on available seats. TTCs also prepare a roster of reserve candidates, usually about 20 percent of trainees. Candidates from this pool replace students who have dropped out during the first 15 days of the semester.

TTCs prioritize applicants who are ethnic minorities, contract teachers, or individuals from remote and disadvantaged areas. These applicants receive extra points on their entrance examination scores. Female applicants do not receive extra points on their examination scores, but are given preference over men with equal scores.

All TTC and NIE courses are designed in accordance with the national curriculum and are required to include modules covering the 2010 teacher standards for their respective subsectors. All year 1 trainees undertake a six-week teaching practice where they observe real classroom teaching, assist teachers, and in a few cases do some teaching themselves. Year 2 trainees undertake an eight-week teaching practicum. To graduate, all trainees must take the final examination in July. Almost all year 2 students pass the exit examination.[2] MoEYS has no accreditation or quality assurance system to measure TTC performance.

TTC Data Collection and Sample Description

The data collection instruments to evaluate teacher preparation (appendix F, available online) were piloted in June 2012 in two TTCs and then adjusted. Teams of enumerators completed the information during two-day school visits.

The Sample

Year 2 enrollment in 2012 was 1,183 for 12+2 students and 784 for 9+2 students (table 2.1). There were 327 PTTC trainers and 224 RTTC trainers.

Our sampling strategy achieves national coverage while allowing for comparisons between disadvantaged and nondisadvantaged areas. The study's focus on year 2 students—who are nearly finished with their training—allows a more powerful sample to assess skills and responses.

We visited 10 TTCs—three RTTCs and seven PTTCs. In the RTTC sample, 301 trainees, or 21.5 percent of the RTTC year 2 population, were interviewed. The seven PTTCs, which included three of the five centers that serve remote and disadvantaged areas, were divided into three groups: PTTCs with 12+2 and 9+2 tranches (three centers), PTTCs with the 12+2 tranche only (three centers), and PTTCs with the 9+2 tranche only (one center). The PTTC sample coverage is extensive—651 of 1,967 trainees (see table 2.1), roughly 33 percent of the population, were interviewed.

The random draw, based on probability proportional to size, helps ensure generalizability to the larger population and sample weights add precision. The weights are constructed based on the number of trainees for each of the four center types (RTTC, then PTTC based on 12+2/9+2 breakdown).

Finally, in each of the 10 TTCs, random samples of 10 trainers completed the survey and mathematics knowledge instruments. The sample—102 trainers, or about 22 percent of PTTC trainers (see table 2.1) and 14 percent of RTTC trainers—provides sufficient power to discuss national averages and compare TTC types.

Findings

The TTCs are adequately equipped, but there are concerns about teacher preparation quality and standardization.

Table 2.1 TTC Population

Location	Number of trainees		Number of trainers
	12+2 program	9+2 program	
Primary teacher training center (PTTC)	1,183	784	327
Banteay Meanchey	29	79	15
Battambang	50	145	33
Kampong Cham	58	100	30
Kampong Chhnang	79	—	14
Kampong Speu	76	—	19
Kampong Thom	68	41	15
Kampot	90	—	19
Kandal	115	4	22
Kratie	74	—	12
Phnom Penh	27	40	31
Preah Vihear	—	84	10
Prey Veng	131	—	22
Pursat	58	—	21
Siem Reap	99	132	29
Sihanouk	50	—	10
Steung Treng	—	159	18
Svay Rieng	60	—	10
Takeo	119	—	17
Lower secondary teacher training center (RTTC)	1,402	—	224
Battambang	343	—	41
Kampong Cham	232	—	41
Kandal	245	—	44
Phnom Penh	218	—	42
Prey Veng	178	—	27
Takeo	186	—	29

Source: World Bank 2012b.
Note: — = these programs are not offered in these TTCs; PTTC = provincial teacher training center; RTTC = regional teacher training center; TTC = teacher training center.

TTC Basic Features

TTCs are well equipped with resources such as libraries and laboratories, but only about half incorporate the new teacher standards (table 2.2). Few TTCs have integrated technology into trainee evaluations or teacher recruitment, limiting opportunities to increase efficiency and prepare teachers and schools for increasing technological demands.

Resources and Laboratories

Perhaps unsurprisingly, RTTCs are better equipped than PTTCs with computers, libraries, and laboratories (tables 2.3–2.5). On average, there are about 23 students to a computer in Cambodian TTCs. This ratio is substantially lower in RTTCs, about 14 students to a computer. Although most TTCs have Internet connections, only half of TTC students can access them. This figure is 25 percent higher in RTTCs.

RTTCs have more laboratories than do PTTCs— an average of 3.5 out of 6 (compared with 1.8 for PTTCs). The RTTCs are also the only TTCs with biology or chemistry labs. Computer laboratories are available in all 10 surveyed TTCs, but the ratio of computers to students is fairly high, suggesting limited access. RTTC students also seem to use laboratories more. Seventy-eight percent of TTCs—and all three of the surveyed RTTCs—report that students are required to take a practicum in the laboratory.

The quality of facilities such as the student computer room also appears to be low (appendix table C.1).

Table 2.2 TTC Descriptive Statistics

Variable	All TTCs	RTTCs	PTTCs All	PTTCs Remote
Total enrollment	397.6	559.2	282.5	373.5
Year 1	195.4	274.0	139.4	189.8
Year 2	202.2	285.0	143.1	183.7
Compound size	41,733	26,148	52,238	86,304
Number of buildings	9.8	10.1	9.5	9.7
Student–trainer ratio	10.4	11.0	10.0	8.6
Use teacher standards	49.6	48.1	50.7	82.8
Sample size (number)	10	3	7	3

Source: World Bank 2012b.
Note: PTTC = provincial teacher training center; RTTC = regional teacher training center; TTC = teacher training center.

Table 2.3 TTC Resources
Percent, unless otherwise indicated

Variable	All TTCs	RTTCs	PTTCs All	PTTCs Remote
Students per computer	23.0	13.8	29.5	21.9
Are following available?				
Printers	100.0	100.0	100.0	100.0
LCD projectors	100.0	100.0	100.0	100.0
Slide projectors	43.6	76.1	20.5	17.2
Overhead projectors	44.0	51.9	38.3	55.5
Photo recorders	100.0	100.0	100.0	100.0
Audiovisual recorders	36.3	76.1	8.0	17.2
Average availability of above resources	70.7	84.0	61.1	65.0
Access to Internet	92.9	100.0	87.8	100.0
For students	46.8	76.1	25.9	55.5
Access to library	100.0	100.0	100.0	100.0
Share of books that are texts	50.3	80.8	33.8	22.4
Sample size (number)	10	3	7	3

Source: World Bank 2012a.
Note: PTTC = provincial teacher training center; RTTC = regional teacher training center; TTC = teacher training center.

Table 2.4 TTC Laboratories

			PTTCs	
Variable	All TTCs	RTTCs	All	Remote
Number of laboratories	2.5	3.5	1.8	1.8
Laboratories by subject (% have):				
Language	0	0	0	0
Computer	100.0	100.0	100.0	100.0
Biology	41.6	100.0	0	0
Chemistry	41.6	100.0	0	0
Social sciences	0	0	0	0
Other	65.6	51.9	75.3	82.3
Hours per month in operation	53.8	48.0	55.0	50.2
Are students required to take practicum in lab? (% yes)	77.8	100.0	62.1	44.5
Sample size (number)	10	3	7	3

Source: World Bank 2012b.
Note: PTTC = provincial teacher training center; RTTC = regional teacher training center; TTC = teacher training center.

Table 2.5 TTC Technology Resources and Policies
Percent, unless otherwise indicated

			PTTCs	
Variable	All TTCs	RTTCs	All	Remote
Have a tech support unit?				
Yes	47.3	48.1	46.7	100.0
Have a policy to promote ICT innovation in teaching?				
Yes	31.9	48.1	20.3	17.2
Are courses in tech skills provided?				
Not provided	7.3	0	12.5	0
Optional	58.3	100.0	28.6	100.0
Mandatory	0	0	0	0
Optional or mandatory, depends on class	34.4	0	58.9	0
Are workshops in technology skills provided?				
Not provided	31.7	48.1	20.0	17.2
Optional	36.3	0	25.2	27.3
Mandatory	9.7	0	16.6	0
Optional or mandatory, depends on class	22.3	51.9	38.1	55.5
Is ICT pedagogical competence stated in course plans?				
Not at all	19.2	0	32.8	44.6
In less than half	60.8	51.9	67.2	55.4
In half	20.3	48.1	0	0
In more than half	0	0	0	0
In all of them	0	0	0	0

table continues next page

Table 2.5 TTC Technology Resources and Policies *(continued)*
Percent, unless otherwise indicated

			PTTCs	
Variable	All TTCs	RTTCs	All	Remote
Does trainer recruitment include ICT assessment?				
Not included at all	61.4	48.1	70.9	100.0
Included, but not decisive	18.9	27.9	12.5	0
Decisive	19.7	23.9	16.6	0
Are students' pedagogical ICT competencies formally assessed?				
Yes	39.0	48.0	33.0	17.2
Sample size (number)	10	3	7	3

Source: World Bank 2012b.
Note: ICT = information and communication technology; PTTC = provincial teacher training center; RTTC = regional teacher training center; TTC = teacher training center.

Technology

TTCs do not use much technology (table 2.5). Less than half have a technology support unit to maintain and operate information and communication technologies (ICTs). Nor does technology play a significant role in coursework or trainee assessment. Only about one-third of surveyed TTCs promote ICT innovation in teaching, and no TTCs have academic departments responsible for technology issues. Most TTCs offer optional—rather than mandatory—courses or workshops involving technological skills, and many offer no such workshops. ICT competencies also play a negligible role in lesson plans, and less than 40 percent of TTCs assess trainee technological competencies. In most TTCs (62 percent), trainer recruitment does not include ICT assessment.

RTTCs use more technology than do PTTCs. The RTTCs are more likely to promote ICT innovation in teaching and marginally more likely to offer courses in these areas. RTTCs report more technology content in course plans, a greater emphasis on technology capacity in recruiting trainers, and more frequent trainee ICT assessment.

These differences between trainer center levels should be understood in context. Given the limitations in technology resources (see table 2.3) it is probably difficult for TTCs to integrate technology into lesson plans, classes, and trainee evaluations. And as with laboratories, TTC conditions may be different from new teachers' actual work sites, especially in rural areas, where schools may lack computers and other technological equipment.

TTC trainers feel that upgraded technological resources would stimulate student interest and lessen the work burden on trainers (appendix F, available online).

Teacher Standards

Both trainers and year 2 trainees express concern about preparation in teacher standards. Though required, teacher standards (box 2.1) are not a part of the curriculum in half of the schools (table 2.6), and trainees are not very comfortable with their preparation in these standards. Less than 10 percent of RTTC

Box 2.1 Teacher Standards in Cambodia

Articulating clear standards for "what makes a good teacher"—such as what a teacher should know and be able to do—is an important step in developing a more professional teaching corps. Cambodia's teacher standards, officially approved in 2010, comprise four domains: professional knowledge, professional practice, professional learning, and professional ethics. Each domain contains several standards specifying observable competencies and behaviors that positively impact student learning. These specifications can be used to assess teacher performance and improve a school's instructional evaluation and planning.

Some competencies address minimum standards, for example, demonstrating commitment and dedication to teaching. Some reflect what most teachers currently do, for example, providing a safe learning environment. Others can only be met by some teachers, for example, using information communications technology and library resources.

The teacher standards were designed to accomplish the following goals in all basic education schools in Cambodia: guide teacher training program reform; help assess teacher training center graduates to ensure they meet minimum standards for accreditation; focus teacher technical meetings and strengthen peer mentoring and instructional supervision by school directors; and establish a clear path for meritorious teacher placement and career advancement, shifting performance evaluations from educational background and years of teaching to observable performance and competency tied to student achievement.

Table 2.6 TTC Trainer Use of Teacher Standards
Percent, unless otherwise indicated

Variable	Full samples		PTTC subsamples		
	RTTC	PTTC	12+2/9+2	12+2	Remote
Aware of teacher standards?					
Yes	33.3	**53.3+**	63.3	43.8	60.2
Do you have a copy?					
Yes	20.0	**43.2***	50.0	37.5	53.6
Have you received training or guidance in teacher standards?					
Yes	23.3	**42.7***	50.0	34.4	47.9
Do the teacher standards reflect best practices?					
Yes	90.0	96.9	94.7	100.0	92.6
How important are the teacher standards at your TTC?					
Don't use/don't know	66.7	46.7	36.7	56.3	39.8
Use a little	3.3	15.6	13.3	15.6	18.7
Use sometimes	20.0	30.9	43.3	21.9	30.5
Use frequently	10.0	6.8	6.7	6.3	11.0
Do you incorporate teacher standards into training activities?					
Yes	23.3	**44.5***	50.0	40.6	45.7

table continues next page

Table 2.6 TTC Trainer Use of Teacher Standards *(continued)*
Percent, unless otherwise indicated

	Full samples		PTTC subsamples		
Variable	RTTC	PTTC	12+2/9+2	12+2	Remote
Do you have materials that use teacher standards?					
Yes	20.0	35.7	40.0	37.5	33.9
Sample size (number)	30	72	30	32	30

Source: World Bank 2012b.
Note: PTTC = provincial teacher training center; RTTC = regional teacher training center; TTC = teacher training center. All results are based on weighted data. Tests of significance are used to make four comparisons: (a) RTTC versus PTTCs (significant differences highlighted in PTTC column); (b) PTTCs with both 12+2/9+2 programs versus other PTTCs; (c) 12+2 TTC averages versus other PTTC averages; and (d) remote PTTCs versus nonremote PTTC averages.
* = Difference in average/percentage is significant at 0.05 level (two-tail); + = Difference in average/percentage is significant at 0.10 level. Boldface also used to highlight significant differences.

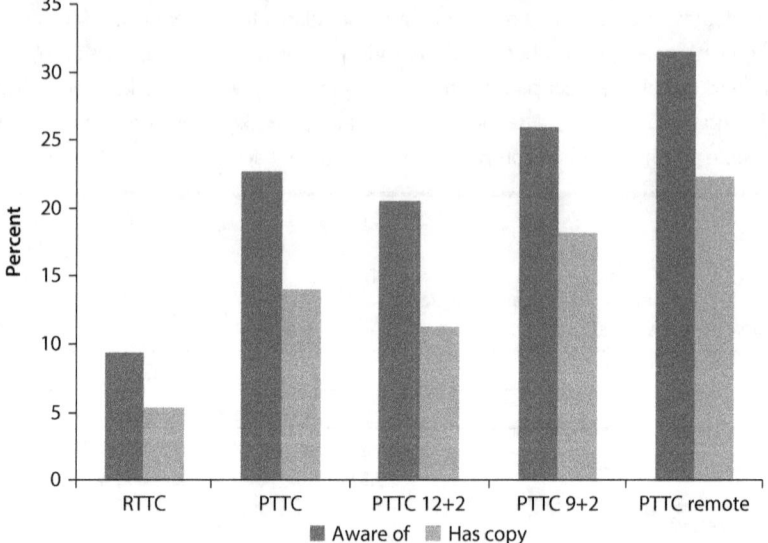

Figure 2.1 Are Trainees Aware of Teacher Standards, and Do They Have a Copy?

Source: World Bank 2012b.
Note: PTTC = provincial teacher training center; RTTC = regional teacher training center.

trainees and 22 percent of PTTC trainees are aware of the teacher standards, and only 5 percent of RTTC trainees and 14 percent of PTTC trainees have a written copy (figure 2.1). In the 9+2 and remote PTTCs, these percentages are only marginally higher.

Only about 40 percent of trainers have heard of the teacher standards—even fewer have a written copy (see table 2.6). PTTC trainers are more likely than their RTTC counterparts to be aware of the standards and have a written copy, but even trainers with a written copy of the standards seldom incorporate them into training. Only 7 percent of PTTC trainers indicated that they use the teacher standards frequently in their classes. The percentage of trainers who had received some guidance in teacher standards is about as low as the percentage with written copies. Teacher standards are not playing a central role in teacher preparation, and much work remains to incorporate them into training.

TTC Trainees

Trainees constitute a fairly homogenous group (table 2.7). The nearly 1,000 year 2 trainees surveyed are young (about 22 years old), not likely to be married, and fairly evenly split by gender. Only about 3 percent identified themselves as a minority (not presented). PTTC trainees are slightly more likely to be female, and remote PTTCs have a significantly lower percentage of females than nonremote PTTCs (54 percent versus about 60 percent). Not surprisingly, RTTC and 12+2 PTTC students have more education than PTTC and 9+2 program participants.

Year 2 trainees feel positive about their preparation, with averages at 3 ("prepared") or above for lesson plans, discipline, teaching methods, curriculum, and evaluation (figure 2.2).

TTC Trainers

RTTC trainers have more education and are better paid than PTTC trainers. Both RTTC and PTTC trainers report a positive working environment and few constraints in preparing teachers. But they have concerns about quality. First, trainer surveys confirm that the new teacher standards play a very minor role in preparing teachers. Many trainers have not heard of the teacher standards, and even trainers with written copies seldom incorporate them into

Table 2.7 TTC Trainees
Percent, unless otherwise indicated

	Full samples		PTTC subsamples		
Variable	RTTC	PTTC	12+2	9+2	Remote
Female	51.2	**57.9***	58.5	57.1	**54.0***
Age (years)	22.2	**21.5***	21.9	**20.8***	21.5
Married	6.6	8.8	7.9	10.3	8.7
Has attended college	24.6	15.7	23.8	**3.2***	**7.1+**
Total education (years)	13.4	**12.5***	13.2	**11.5***	12.1
Pre-TTC train course	14.6	13.7	12.9	14.8	16.0
Contract teaching experience	13.6	**5.9+**	5.8	6.1	8.0
Sample size (number)	301	651	387	264	257

Source: World Bank 2012b.
Note: PTTC = provincial teacher training center; RTTC = regional teacher training center; TTC = teacher training center. All results are based on weighted data. Tests of significance are used to compare RTTC and PTTC averages (significant differences highlighted in PTTC column), 12+2 and 9+2 averages (significant differences highlighted in 9+2 column), and remote and nonremote PTTC averages (highlighted in remote column).
* = Difference in average/percentage is significant at 0.05 level (two-tail); + = Difference in average/percentage is significant at 0.10 level. Boldface also used to highlight significant differences.

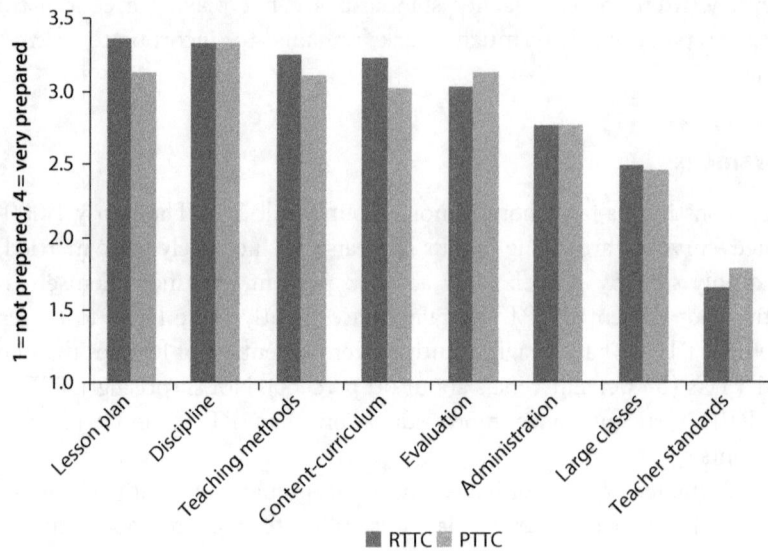

Figure 2.2 Trainee Self-Reported Level of Preparation for Teaching, RTTC-PTTC

Source: World Bank 2012b.
Note: PTTC = provincial teacher training center; RTTC = regional teacher training center.

their classes. There is a major disconnect between the MoEYS teacher training goals, the stated curricular guidelines, and what is happening in TTC classrooms.

Second, trainers work in an environment with little contact, support, or collaboration. Trainers report little contact with other teachers, few visits from directors, and little input from the Provincial Offices of Education about their classroom work. Such isolation, especially without well-defined mechanisms to assess training effectiveness (such as visits from the teacher training department), can be problematic.

Trainer Background and Education

TTC trainers (table 2.8) average about 36 years of age and are more likely to be female and married; 100 percent reported being Khmer ethnicity (not reported in table). Most live within 30 minutes of the TTC and have a motorbike, and a small number (less than 10 percent) live on site.

Most TTC trainers come from the teaching profession. About 70 percent are former teachers, and another 10 percent are former school directors (table 2.9). About 15 percent do not report working previously as teachers or directors, but the translated responses for "other" indicate that most were deputy directors, librarians, and heads of technical groups (presumably in schools).

Most TTC trainers also have education beyond high school, and RTTC trainers are more educated than their PTTC counterparts (see table 2.9). RTTC trainers report 16.5 years of study, corresponding to university-educated (though this figure may count training activities as full years of study). For PTTC trainers the

Table 2.8 TTC Trainers
Percent, unless otherwise indicated

	Full samples		PTTC subsamples		
Variable	RTTC	PTTC	12+2/9+2	12+2	Remote
Female	70.0	55.8	50.0	56.3	60.9
Age (years)	34.4	36.2	36.9	36.5	36.1
Married	63.3	73.1	70.0	**81.3***	69.2
Number of children	1.0	**1.7***	1.6	**2.1***	1.5
Time to travel to center					
Stay in TTC	10.0	6.3	0	9.4	6.4
1–15 minutes	36.7	67.3	73.3	59.4	71.0
16–30 minutes	36.7	20.5	20.0	25.0	18.2
30–60 minutes	13.3	4.7	6.7	3.1	4.4
More than 60 minutes	3.3	1.3	0	3.1	0
Sig (*p*-value)	*p* = 0.25		*p* = 0.53	*p* = 0.82	*p* = 0.68
Have motorbike or car	86.2	71.7	69.0	77.4	91.2

Source: World Bank 2012b.
Note: PTTC = provincial teacher training center; RTTC = regional teacher training center; TTC = teacher training center. All results are based on weighted data. Tests of significance are used to make four comparisons: RTTC versus PTTC averages (significant differences highlighted in PTTC column); PTTCs with both 12+2/9+2 programs versus other PTTCs; 12+2 TTC averages versus other PTTC averages; and remote PTTCs versus nonremote PTTC averages.
* = Difference in average/percentage is significant at 0.05 level (two-tail); + = Difference in average/percentage is significant at 0.10 level. Boldface also used to highlight significant differences.

Table 2.9 TTC Trainer Background and Education
Percent, unless otherwise indicated

	Full samples		PTTC subsamples		
Variable	RTTC	PTTC	12+2/9+2	12+2	Remote
Teacher type					
Head teacher	10.0	12.2	13.3	9.4	13.2
Full time (teacher)	76.7	64.9	56.7	71.9	55.4
Temporary/probation	0	4.7	6.7	3.1	8.9
Other	13.3	18.3	23.3	15.6	22.6
Highest LSS grade					
LSS 7	23.3	35.8	33.3	43.8	27.1
LSS 8	30.0	14.0	15.3	15.6	17.9
LSS 9	46.7	50.2	53.3	40.6	55.0
Highest USS grade					
Did not attend	3.3	25.0	30.0	21.9	24.7
USS 10	13.3	7.3	6.7	9.4	0
USS 11	30.0	12.8	10.0	18.8	19.2
USS 12	53.3	54.9	53.3	50.0	56.1
Attended university?	93.3	**66.7***	66.7	71.9	70.1

table continues next page

Table 2.9 TTC Trainer Background and Education *(continued)*
Percent, unless otherwise indicated

	Full samples		PTTC subsamples		
Variable	RTTC	PTTC	12+2/9+2	12+2	Remote
Total years of study (years)	16.5	**14.7***	14.6	14.8	14.8
Sample size (number)	30	72	30	32	30

Source: World Bank 2012b.
Note: LSS = lower secondary school; PTTC = provincial teacher training center; RTTC = regional teacher training center; TTC = teacher training center; USS = upper secondary school. All results are based on weighted data. Tests of significance are used to make four comparisons: RTTC versus PTTC averages (significant differences highlighted in PTTC column); PTTCs with both 12+2/9+2 programs versus other PTTCs; 12+2 TTC averages versus other PTTC averages; and remote PTTCs versus nonremote PTTC averages.
* = Difference in average/percentage is significant at 0.05 level (two-tail); + = Difference in average/percentage is significant at 0.10 level. Boldface also used to highlight significant differences.

Table 2.10 Training and Work Experiences

	Full samples		PTTC subsamples		
Variable	RTTC	PTTC	12+2/9+2	12+2	Remote
Completed preservice teacher training	90.0	97.4	100.0	93.8	100.0
1-year program	88.9	45.8	46.7	50.0	39.2
2-year program	7.4	32.1	26.7	33.3	37.4
3+ year program	3.7	22.1	26.7	16.7	23.4
Sig (p-value)		$p = 0.00$	$p = 0.75$	$p = 0.34$	$p = 0.38$
Completed inservice teacher training (this year)	56.7	**86.3***	**96.7+**	**75.0+**	85.5
Quality of training					
Average	76.5	48.5	51.7	54.2	58.7
Very good	23.5	51.5	48.3	45.8	41.3
Sig (p-value)		$p = 0.01$	$p = 0.97$	$p = 0.76$	$p = 0.28$
Years as teacher	10.4	**13.8+**	14.1	14.8	12.9
Had leadership role in school?	23.3	27.9	**36.7***	**18.8+**	29.9
Worked in NGO?	33.3	**15.3+**	10.0	18.8	14.3
Attended trainer training?	13.3	11.6	**3.3***	**21.9+**	9.0
Sample size (number)	30	72	30	32	30

Source: World Bank 2012b.
Note: NGO = nongovernmental organization; PTTC = provincial teacher training center; RTTC = regional teacher training center. All results are based on weighted data. Tests of significance are used to make four comparisons: RTTC versus PTTC averages (significant differences highlighted in PTTC column); PTTCs with both 12+2/9+2 programs versus other PTTCs; 12+2 TTC averages versus other PTTC averages; and remote PTTCs versus nonremote PTTC averages.
* = Difference in average/percentage is significant at 0.05 level (two-tail); + = Difference in average/percentage is significant at 0.10 level. Boldface also used to highlight significant differences.

average is 14.7 years, suggesting completion of upper secondary plus some additional university study.

Most TTC trainers attended a teacher trainer program, although 10 percent of RTTC trainers had no formal teacher training (table 2.10). PTTC trainers had longer preservice training; more RTTC trainers attended a one-year program.

Table 2.11 TTC Trainer Salaries
Thousands of riel per month, unless otherwise indicated

	Full samples		PTTC subsamples		
Variable	RTTC	PTTC	12+2/9+2	12+2	Remote
Total salary	623.8	**509.5***	512.7	508.1	506.1
Baseline salary	559.7	**457.4***	452.2	**475.9+**	458.4
Overtime	63.7	44.7	56.1	31.4	33.1
Remote posting	0	4.8	0	0	12.8
Good teaching award	0.2	0.4	0.6	0.3	0.8
Other incentive	0.1	2.2	3.9	0.7	1.1
Paid facilitation fee? (%)	16.7	30.5	46.7	**3.1***	41.6
Absences per year (%)					
0 days	6.7	4.7	0	9.4	2.1
1–10 days	73.3	66.2	56.7	75.0	57.8
11–30 days	13.3	27.5	40.0	15.6	35.6
30–50 days	6.7	1.7	3.3	0	4.4
Sig (*p*-value)		*p* = 0.39	***p* = 0.01***	***p* = 0.05***	*p* = 0.31
Sample size (number)	30	72	30	32	30

Source: World Bank 2012b.
Note: PTTC = provincial teacher training center; RTTC = regional teacher training center. TTC = teacher training center. All results are based on weighted data. Tests of significance are used to make four comparisons: RTTC versus PTTC averages (significant differences highlighted in PTTC column); PTTCs with both 12+2/9+2 programs versus other PTTCs; 12+2 TTC averages versus other PTTC averages; and remote PTTCs versus nonremote PTTC averages.
* = Difference in average/percentage is significant at 0.05 level (two-tail); + = Difference in average/percentage is significant at 0.10 level. Boldface also used to highlight significant differences.

PTTC trainers also receive more support in the workplace—86.3 percent attended inservice training during the current school year, compared with just 56.7 percent of RTTC trainers. PTTC training is also reported to be better than RTTC training. Roughly one-third of RTTC trainers worked for a nongovernmental organization, versus only about 15 percent of PTTC trainers, indicating greater preparation among RTTC staff.

TTC Trainer Salaries

RTTC trainers receive higher monthly salaries than PTTC trainers by an average of about 114,000 riel, or $25 (table 2.11), mainly because of higher base salaries and more overtime pay. As expected, remote TTC trainers receive slightly more pay for the remote posting (about 12,000 riel, or $3).

On average, about 17 percent of RTTC trainers and 31 percent of PTTC trainers pay facilitation fees to receive their salaries. The trainers report missing between 0 and 10 days a year (self-reported absences), though a substantial proportion of PTTC trainers report missing between 11 and 30 days. The most commonly cited reasons for absences are personal and work- or training-related.

TTC Work Experiences

Less than half of teacher trainers consider trainees prepared for training (table 2.12). More RTTC trainers consider this lack of preparation a

Table 2.12 Trainer Opinions about Training Constraints
Percent, unless otherwise indicated

	Full samples		PTTC subsamples		
Variable	RTTC	PTTC	12+2/9+2	12+2	Remote
Preparation of teacher trainees					
Not a constraint	43.3	40.8	40.0	43.8	44.7
Minor constraint	36.7	52.1	50.0	53.1	44.3
Major constraint	20.0	7.2	10.0	3.1	11.0
Time available to provide training					
Not a constraint	50.0	50.4	46.7	53.1	60.0
Minor constraint	43.3	35.7	36.7	37.5	15.6
Major constraint	6.7	13.9	16.7	9.4	24.4
Classroom materials					
Not a constraint	26.7	30.0	43.3	15.6	25.5
Minor constraint	36.7	59.9	50.0	71.9	65.8
Major constraint	36.7	10.2	6.7	12.5	8.7
Laboratory facilities					
Not a constraint	60.0	45.1	46.7	50.0	35.6
Minor constraint	26.7	33.9	36.7	31.3	30.0
Major constraint	13.3	21.0	16.7	18.7	34.4
Applied teaching experiences for trainees					
Not a constraint	60.0	67.1	63.3	75.0	65.7
Minor constraint	36.7	28.6	33.3	18.8	26.4
Major constraint	3.3	4.3	3.3	6.3	7.9
Training level of teacher trainers					
Not a constraint	26.7	39.1	36.7	43.8	30.0
Minor constraint	56.7	54.6	53.3	53.1	65.6
Major constraint	16.7	6.3	10.0	3.1	4.4
Sample size (number)	30	72	30	32	30

Source: World Bank 2012b.
Note: PTTC = provincial teacher training center; RTTC = regional teacher training center. All results are based on weighted data. Tests of significance are used to make four comparisons: RTTC versus PTTC averages (significant differences highlighted in PTTC column); PTTCs with both 12+2/9+2 programs versus other PTTCs; 12+2 TTC averages versus other PTTC averages; and remote PTTCs versus nonremote PTTC averages.
* = Difference in average/percentage is significant at 0.05 level (two-tail); + = Difference in average/percentage is significant at 0.10 level. Boldface also used to highlight significant differences.

major constraint. Teacher trainers do not feel constrained by time or lack of applied teaching experiences. They express concerns about their own preparation for training trainees and about the availability of classroom materials, especially in the RTTCs, where 36.7 percent of trainers indicated that lack of materials was a major constraint. Concerns about resources do not include laboratories, as 60 percent of RTTC trainers and 45 percent of PTTC trainers indicated that labs were not a constraint.

Figure 2.3 Teacher-Reported Problems in TTCs

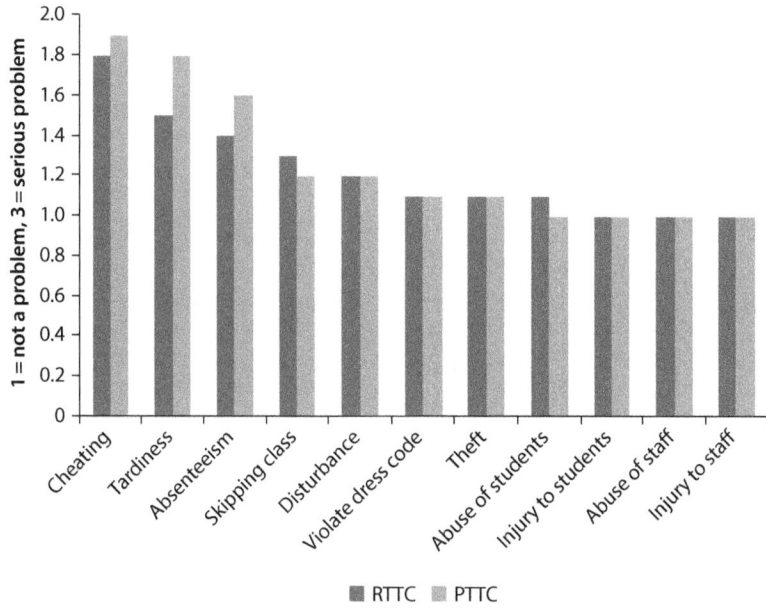

Source: World Bank 2012b.
Note: PTTC = provincial teacher training center; RTTC = regional teacher training center; TTC = teacher training center.

Teacher trainers are moderately concerned about cheating, tardiness, and absenteeism (figure 2.3), but they do not report many other problems in their workplaces.

There is little TTC trainer interaction and support (table 2.13), consistent with previous studies suggesting that teacher trainers operate with limited support from directors or collaboration with other teachers (Benveniste, Marshall, and Aranjo 2008).

Almost all TTC trainers have technical meetings (covering teaching methods, lesson planning, and how to improve student learning) and most attend these meetings regularly (see table 2.13), but school directors are largely absent, particularly in RTTCs. Many RTTC directors (about 25 percent) do not attend the technical meetings. And only about 30 percent of RTTC trainers, compared with 70 percent of PTTC trainers, agreed that their director is "available and approachable." PTTC directors are significantly more likely than RTTC directors to observe trainers in their classrooms: 31.9 percent of PTTC trainers, versus only 10 percent of RTTC trainers, report being observed by the director at least once a month.

PTTC trainers also visit other classrooms to observe instruction more frequently than their RTTC counterparts, although the number of these visits is fairly low. Contact with teacher training personnel is also infrequent. TTCs thus seem to be isolated from classroom realities.

Table 2.13 TTC Trainer Interaction and Support
Percent, unless otherwise indicated

	Full samples		PTTC subsamples		
Variable	RTTC	PTTC	12+2/9+2	12+2	Remote
TTC has technical meetings	93.3	100.0	100.0	100.0	100.0
Never/rarely attend	10.7	2.6	0	6.3	3.4
Usually attend	32.1	23.8	23.3	25.0	36.8
Always attend	57.1	73.7	76.7	68.8	59.8
Sig (*p*-value)	*p* = 0.16		*p* = 0.60	*p* = 0.48	**_p_ = 0.05***
Does the director attend?					
Never/rarely	25.9	9.3	10.0	6.3	17.6
Usually	22.2	35.2	26.7	40.6	32.0
Always	51.9	55.6	63.3	53.1	50.5
Sig (*p*-value)	*p* = 0.35		*p* = 0.37	*p* = 0.92	*p* = 0.37
Primary activities					
Teaching methodology	40.7	42.2	53.6	25.0	42.8
Lesson planning	18.5	16.6	3.6	34.4	8.0
How to improve learning	11.1	16.4	10.7	21.9	20.4
Administrative	11.1	7.1	7.2	6.3	5.7
Other	18.5	17.7	25.0	12.5	23.1
How often do you visit other classrooms?					
Never	**80.0**	**55.2**	43.3	**68.8**	**50.1**
Almost never	20.0	23.2	30.0	15.6	29.9
Monthly	0	13.5	20.0	6.3	6.6
Weekly/daily	0	8.1	6.6	9.4	13.4
Sig (*p*-value)	**_p_ = 0.06+**		**_p_ = 0.03***	**_p_ = 0.04***	*p* = 0.55
How often does the director observe you?					
Never	**36.7**	19.5	20.0	18.8	20.0
Once per year	16.7	16.0	16.7	12.5	15.3
Every six months	20.0	14.0	20.0	9.4	4.4
Every three months	16.7	18.7	20.0	18.8	10.0
At least once per month	10.0	31.9	23.3	40.6	50.3
Sig (*p*-value)	**_p_ = 0.01***		*p* = 0.28	*p* = 0.30	*p* = 0.17
Is your director available and approachable?	32.1	**69.3***	76.7	56.3	**86.6***
How often does the teacher training department observe you?					
Never	**53.3**	27.8	26.7	25.0	30.8
Once per year	26.7	35.0	46.7	21.9	34.4
Every six months	16.7	27.8	20.0	40.6	28.2
Every three months	3.3	9.4	6.7	12.5	6.6
Sig (*p*-value)	*p* = 0.15		*p* = 0.22	**_p_ = 0.04***	*p* = 0.53
Sample size (number)	30	72	30	32	30

Source: World Bank 2012b.
Note: PTTC = provincial teacher training center; RTTC = regional teacher training center; TTC = teacher training center. All results are based on weighted data. Tests of significance are used to make four comparisons: RTTC versus PTTC averages (significant differences highlighted in PTTC column); PTTCs with both 12+2/9+2 programs versus other PTTCs; 12+2 TTC averages versus other PTTC averages; and remote PTTCs versus nonremote PTTC averages.
* = Difference in average/percentage is significant at 0.05 level (two-tail); + = Difference in average/percentage is significant at 0.10 level. Boldface also used to highlight significant differences.

Classroom Observations

To gain a more detailed picture of teacher preparation, we observed two classes in each of the 10 TTCs (20 classes in all). Questionnaires investigated attendance, lesson planning, teaching activities, and time segments to see how TTC classes are structured. The results suggest that TTC classes are well organized, have a sequential coherence, and involve some minimal teacher–student interaction. But the teaching and learning environment in the average TTC is teacher-centered and far from interactive, raising concerns about instruction quality.

Attendance and Lesson Plans

In about 25 percent of the visited classrooms, teachers do not report taking student attendance, and in another 16 percent, teachers report taking attendance but could not produce an attendance book (table 2.14). The observed—as opposed to trainer-reported—trainee attendance rate averaged about 80 percent during the school visits (much lower in the 9+2 and remote TTCs). This low attendance rate raises serious questions about the program's demands.

In most of the observed classes (about 87 percent), the trainer could produce a written lesson plan for that day's work, suggesting some preparation and thus teaching quality.

Classroom Time Segments

In each of the 20 observed classes, we applied a time segment instrument that divided the class time into four categories: class management, instruction activities, recitation, and work activities (table 2.15). Each category contains 2–4 subcategories. Class time averaged about 52 minutes, slightly less than the official time designated.

Table 2.14 Attendance and Lesson Plans
Percent, unless otherwise indicated

				PTTCs		
Variable	All TTCs	RTTCs	PTTCs	12+2	9+2	Remote
Does teacher take attendance?						
No	**26.6**	37.9	18.6	**50.0**	0	8.6
Yes, but is not present	15.8	0	27.1	22.4	100.0	27.3
Yes, and is present	57.6	62.1	54.4	27.6	0	64.1
Number of trainees	22.9	19.2	26.2	19.2	18.0	37.4
Attendance rate (scale of 0–100)	81.3	87.4	76.1	82.1	24.9	67.1
Lesson plan written out?	86.7	100.0	77.1	89.2	**0**	64.1
Sample size (number)	20	6	14	6	2	6

Source: World Bank 2012b.
Note: PTTC = provincial teacher training center; RTTC = regional teacher training center; TTC = teacher training center. All results are based on weighted data. Because of small sample sizes, tests of significance are not used to make comparisons.

Table 2.15 Class Time Use
Percentage of total class time, unless otherwise indicated

				PTTCs		
Variable	All TTCs	RTTCs	PTTCs	12+2	9+2	Remote
Official class length (minutes)	56.3	57.7	55.8	57.4	60.0	55.0
Actual class length (minutes)	52.5	54.4	51.2	55.4	56.0	50.5
Breakdown by activity						
Class management	9.9	10.8	9.3	10.7	4.2	9.2
Get control	2.9	3.3	2.7	2.5	1.0	3.7
No instruction	7.0	7.5	6.6	8.2	3.2	5.5
Instruction activities	39.4	45.8	34.8	39.4	68.0	30.2
Teacher instruction	23.0	20.9	24.5	29.8	39.8	21.0
Students copying	13.9	**24.7**	6.2	1.5	**26.9**	8.7
Students reading	2.5	0.2	4.1	8.1	2.3	0.6
Recitation	23.1	17.8	26.8	30.5	20.9	24.7
Question-answer	16.3	12.4	19.1	20.0	15.1	16.3
Student asking	0.9	1.2	0.6	1.6	0	0.3
Student receiving answer	5.9	4.2	7.1	8.9	5.8	8.1
Work activities	27.5	25.4	29.1	19.3	5.8	35.8
Seatwork	3.3	5.6	1.7	1.3	0	2.8
Discussion	6.6	5.4	7.5	2.5	3.3	7.5
Group work	16.1	14.4	17.3	15.5	0	19.9
Kinesthetics	1.5	0	2.6	0	2.5	5.6
Sample size (number)	20	6	14	6	2	6

Source: World Bank 2012b.
Note: PTTC = provincial teacher training center; RTTC = regional teacher training center; TTC = teacher training center. All results are based on weighted data. Because of small sample sizes, tests of significance are not used to comparisons.

About 10 percent of observed class time was spent in class management (getting control of the class or no instruction) and about 40 percent in instruction, including teachers speaking and giving instructions and students copying instructions. Some of these activities, such as dictating and copying lessons, are teacher centric, but these activities are mixed with others. The differences between TTC categories merit attention, especially the very high percentage devoted to instruction in the 9+2 PTTCs.

Student work, including (individual) seatwork and group discussion, made up about 28 percent (or 15 minutes) of class time, and group work took up about 16 percent.

Recitation activities on average took up about one-quarter of the class (figure 2.4). These activities consisted mostly of question and answer exchanges where the teacher asked students to comment. Less frequently, students asked teachers to comment.

The classroom time segment observations were divided into three 20-minute periods in each class (figure 2.5). Not surprisingly, class management was more prevalent at the beginning and end of the class time, as was instruction—the lack

Figure 2.4 Teaching Activities by Category

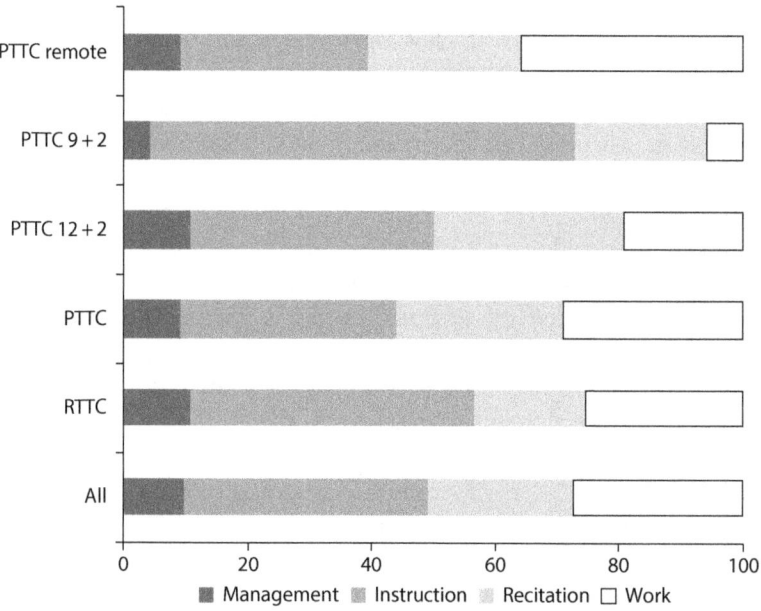

Source: World Bank 2012b.
Note: PTTC = provincial teacher training center; RTTC = regional teacher training center.

Figure 2.5 Time Use Segments by Lesson Period (1–3)

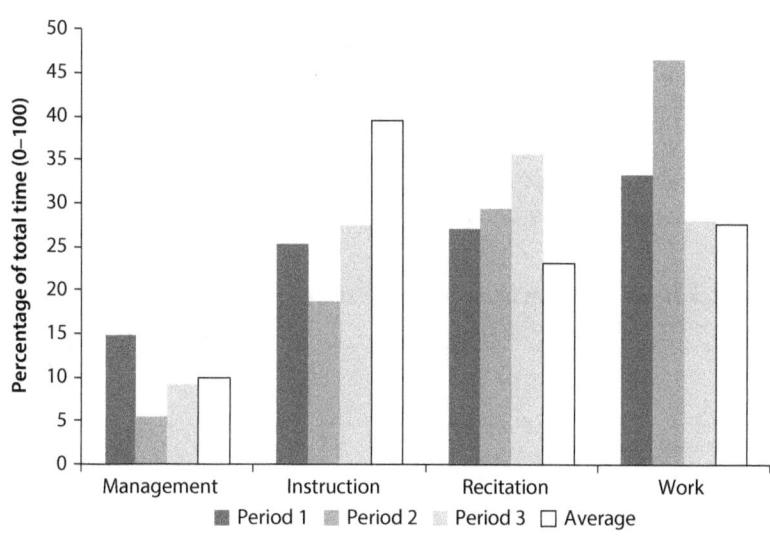

Source: World Bank 2012b.

of instruction in period 2 was at least partially made up for by more work. Recitation averages slowly climb from period 1 to period 3.

The average class begins with class management and then focuses on teacher instruction (see table 2.15 and figure 2.5). In the middle of the lesson, students devote more time to working on individual or group activities. The lesson concludes with instruction and recitation, made up mainly of teacher-initiated question and answer.

Is this good teaching? A definitive answer requires more extensive observation and expertise (preferably using videos). The observed classes include a positive mixture of activities, with some instruction, work time, and recitation. Their sequencing—as measured by the percentages in three 20-minute periods—suggests lesson coherence, with instruction followed by working and concluding with more instruction and recitation. Although these are positive developments, they do not guarantee high-quality teaching.

Teaching Activities

Post-lesson summaries provided by enumerators raise several concerns, such as a lack of learning materials (table 2.16).

Teacher–student interaction is prevalent and consistent with the time segment summaries (table 2.17). Teacher trainers were more likely to ask individual than whole-class ("chorus") questions. In about half of the classes the trainers asked questions requiring students to use imagination or creativity, suggesting that in the other half the question-and-answer interaction focused one dimensionally on facts. In only about one-third of the classrooms did teacher trainees ask the trainers questions, again suggesting a fairly teacher-centered dynamic.

Many teacher trainers (35 percent) do not use praise or encouragement (see table 2.17); 37 percent of trainers never asked their students to provide an opinion, reinforcing teacher-centered instruction.

In almost half of the classrooms, the teacher trainer wrote the lesson on the board from a textbook (table 2.18). This may explain the frequency of copying in RTTCs, which in turn may indicate insufficient learning materials. Ideally, trainees would be able to use materials with lessons already written down.

Table 2.16 Teaching Materials (Classroom Observations)
Percent, unless otherwise indicated

Variable	All TTCs	RTTCs	PTTCs	PTTCs 12+2	PTTCs 9+2	PTTCs Remote
Teacher trainer used teaching aids	41.2	38.0	43.4	16.8	0	27.7
Teacher trainee used textbooks	33.0	50.0	20.8	22.4	50.0	13.7
% of teacher trainees with a textbook	15.5	24.6	0	0	0	0
Displays that are made by teacher trainee	51.3	57.1	47.1	48.9	59.7	37.5
Sample size (number)	20	6	14	6	2	6

Source: World Bank 2012b.
Note: PTTC = provincial teacher training center; RTTC = regional teacher training center; TTC = teacher training center. All results are based on weighted data. Because of small sample sizes, tests of significance are not used to make comparisons.

Table 2.17 Questions and Feedback (Classroom Observations)
Percent, unless otherwise indicated

Variable	All TTCs	RTTCs	PTTCs	PTTCs 12+2	PTTCs 9+2	PTTCs Remote
Teacher trainer question types						
Collectively ("chorus")	46.6	12.0	71.3	56.0	50.0	69.1
Individually	100.0	100.0	100.0	100.0	100.0	100.0
That require imagination	46.3	25.9	60.8	61.6	100.0	55.1
Teacher trainee ask questions?	33.0	38.0	29.5	10.8	50.0	50.0
Teacher trainer feedback						
Praise or encouragement						
Never	35.0	25.9	41.5	78.4	50.0	13.7
Once	17.3	36.0	4.0	10.8	0	8.6
More than once	47.7	38.0	54.5	10.8	50.0	77.7
Correcting a mistake						
Never	20.6	12.0	26.8	56.0	0	0
Once	25.7	36.0	18.3	33.2	0	8.6
More than once	53.7	52.0	54.9	10.8	100.0	91.4
Scolding or critical						
Never	87.5	88.0	87.0	100.0	100.0	72.3
Once	0	0	0	0	0	0
More than once	12.5	12.0	13.0	0	0	27.7
Asked to give opinion						
Never	**36.9**	**36.0**	**37.5**	**50.0**	0	33.3
Once	0	0	0	0	0	0
More than once	63.1	64.0	62.5	50.0	100.0	66.7
Sample size (number)	20	6	14	6	2	6

Source: World Bank 2012b.
Note: PTTC = provincial teacher training center; RTTC = regional teacher training center; TTC = teacher training center. All results are based on weighted data. Because of small sample sizes, tests of significance are not used to make comparisons.

Table 2.18 Work Activities
Percent, unless otherwise indicated

Variable	All TTCs	RTTCs	PTTCs	PTTCs 12+2	PTTCs 9+2	PTTCs Remote
Blackboard used by						
Only teacher	18.7	0	31.9	16.8	100.0	55.1
Teacher and students	81.3	100.0	68.1	83.2	0	44.9
Teacher trainer copied lesson from text onto board	44.8	76.1	22.6	44.4	0	8.6
Teacher trainer summarized lesson/explanation/ discussion on board	83.9	100.0	72.5	60.8	100.0	72.3
Teacher trainer wrote questions on board to copy						
Never	26.7	50.0	10.1	10.8	0	8.6
Once	48.9	38.0	56.6	50.0	0	64.1
More than once	24.4	12.0	33.3	39.2	100.0	27.3

table continues next page

Table 2.18 Work Activities *(continued)*
Percent, unless otherwise indicated

				PTTCs		
Variable	All TTCs	RTTCs	PTTCs	12+2	9+2	Remote
Teacher trainer had trainees carry out task to demonstrate learning of lesson						
Never	20.9	12.0	27.3	39.2	100.0	27.3
Once	12.4	24.1	4.0	10.8	0	8.6
More than once	66.7	64.0	68.7	50.0	0	64.1
Teacher trainer used trainees' names						
Never	24.5	24.1	24.8	66.8	0	8.6
Rarely	11.1	0	19.1	0	0	27.7
Usually	55.0	75.9	40.0	22.4	100.0	55.1
Always	9.4	0	16.1	10.8	0	8.6
Sample size (number)	20	6	14	6	2	6

Source: World Bank 2012b.
Note: PTTC = provincial teacher training center; RTTC = regional teacher training center; TTC = teacher training center. All results are based on weighted data. Because of small sample sizes, tests of significance are not used to make comparisons.

In about 79 percent of the classes, teacher trainers asked the trainees to demonstrate their learning of the lesson, often more than once. Most teachers are thus taking into account how well their students are learning the content, but many classes still lack such verification, raising questions about lesson quality.

Notes

1. Upper secondary school graduates are known as 12+2 graduates and lower secondary school graduates as 9+2 graduates. In 2010, TTCs began admitting 9+2 graduates into its programs in an attempt to staff schools in areas with a dearth of upper secondary graduates.
2. The exceptions are usually trainees who could not fully participate in teaching practice and who are thus not eligible to take the final examination, or those who drop out after securing alternative employment.

Bibliography

Benveniste, Luis, Jeffery Marshall, and M. Caridad Aranjo. 2008. *Teaching in Cambodia.* Washington, DC: World Bank.

Darling-Hammond, Linda. 2000. "Teacher Quality and Student Achievement." *Education Policy Analysis Archives* 8 (1): 1–44.

World Bank 2012a. "Teacher Survey." World Bank, Washington, DC.

———. 2012b. "Teacher Training College Survey." World Bank, Washington, DC.

CHAPTER 3

How Are Teachers Placed?

Key Messages

The teacher placement system considers trainees' geographic preferences, places of residence, and exit examination scores. In choosing schools, trainees prioritize proximity to family and working in their home provinces. Almost all trainees feel that exit examination scores influence their placement, and almost half feel that personal contacts also play a role. Teachers largely agree.

Staffing remote schools is a major challenge. Less than 20 percent of regional teacher training center (RTTC) trainees and only 33 percent of provincial teacher training center (PTTC) trainees state a willingness to work in a remote school, mostly because of the distance and the low salary. The placement bonus has not stimulated interest in teaching in these schools. To be effective, it must be raised and better advertised. Also, because of the importance of proximity to family, local recruitment may help staff remote schools.

Placement Process

The teacher placement system considers trainees' geographic preferences, places of residence, and exit examination scores. Before training, trainees identify the provinces where they will teach after graduation. Once they complete the course and pass the final examination, they choose up to three schools in their selected provinces, of which they are assigned one. Trainees from remote and disadvantaged areas are required to return to their hometowns. Others may choose any schools in their selected provinces. Trainees with high final examination scores are allowed to choose schools first. The placement system does not systematically match supply and demand. All preprimary, primary, and lower secondary trainees become teachers. Only about three to five upper secondary trainees find other jobs.

Placement Factors

In choosing schools, trainees prioritize proximity to family and working in their home provinces, followed by working in an urban area (figure 3.1). Although relevant, going where they are needed or knowing the director/school are

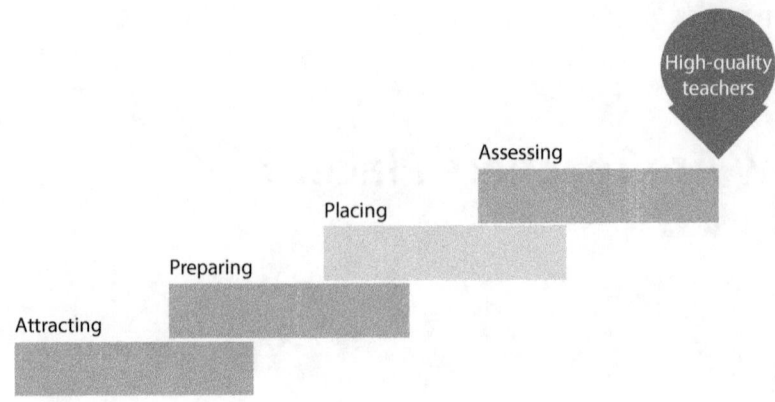

Figure 3.1 Trainee Priorities for School Placement

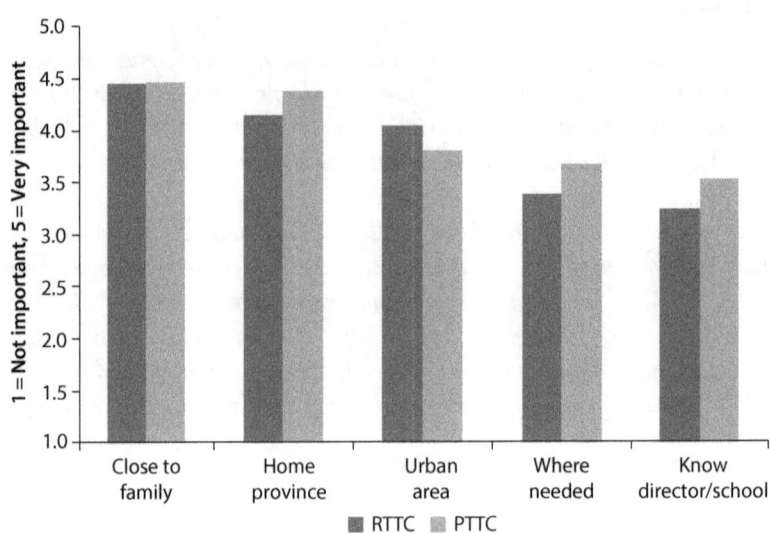

Source: World Bank 2012b.
Note: PTTC = provincial teacher training center; RTTC = regional teacher training center.

less important. These priorities reinforce a common theme in Cambodian teacher policy circles: the importance of proximity to family support networks.

Roughly 97 percent of year 2 trainees (in every teacher training center [TTC] category) feel their scores on the exit exam will be "very important" in determining where they are placed (table 3.1). Almost half of year 2 trainees also feel that personal contacts in schools, district offices of education (DOEs), and provincial offices of education (POEs) will be "very important." Encouragingly, about 80 percent of the surveyed students feel that facilitation fees are "not important" in determining placement. Trainee responses vary little across program and TTC category.

Primary teachers largely confirm trainees' beliefs that exit exam scores and TTC marks are the most important factors in determining placement.

Table 3.1 Trainee Evaluation of Factors Determining Work Place
Percent, unless otherwise indicated

Variable	Full samples		PTTC subsamples		
	RTTC	PTTC	12+2	9+2	Remote
Exit examination score					
Not important	0.7	0.0	0.0	0.0	0.0
Somewhat important	2.3	2.7	2.4	3.1	2.4
Very important	**97.0**	**97.3**	**97.6**	**96.9**	**97.6**
TTC marks					
Not important	0.7	0.3	0.5	0.0	0.0
Somewhat important	18.6	14.4	11.8	18.3	14.9
Very important	80.7	85.3	87.6	81.7	85.1
Contacts in school					
Not important	16.9	20.5	20.6	20.3	21.4
Somewhat important	27.9	30.9	31.7	29.6	22.9
Very important	**55.2**	**48.7**	**47.7**	**50.1**	**55.7**
Contacts at DOE					
Not important	14.3	26.3	24.9	28.4	24.0
Somewhat important	31.2	30.0	32.6	25.9	22.9
Very important	54.5	43.8	42.5	45.8	53.2
Contacts at POE					
Not important	14.6	25.9	24.5	28.0	23.7
Somewhat important	29.9	32.2	33.9	29.5	26.1
Very important	55.5	42.0	41.6	42.5	50.2
Paying facilitation fee					
Not important	77.7	81.6	78.8	85.8	84.9
Somewhat important	16.3	15.6	18.3	11.4	10.9
Very important	6.0	2.9	2.9	2.8	4.2
Where there is a need					
Not important	29.9	16.6	19.4	12.2	11.0
Somewhat important	19.9	25.0	28.3	19.9	21.3
Very important	50.2	58.4	52.3	67.9	67.7
Sample size (number)	301	651	387	264	257

Source: World Bank 2012b.
Note: DOE = district office of education; POE = provincial office of education; PTTC = provincial teacher training center; RTTC = regional teacher training center; TTC = teacher training center. All results are based on weighted data. Tests of significance are not incorporated, but are available upon request. Boldfaced values highlight information discussed in the text.

These factors are followed by "where there is a need" and contacts with various school, DOE, and POE personnel (figure 3.2).

Placement Incentives

Staffing remote schools is a major challenge in Cambodia. Less than 20 percent of RTTC trainees and only 33 percent of PTTC trainees say they would even consider working in a remote school (table 3.2). And trainees in remote PTTCs

Figure 3.2 Teachers and PTTC Trainees on Factors that Influence Placement

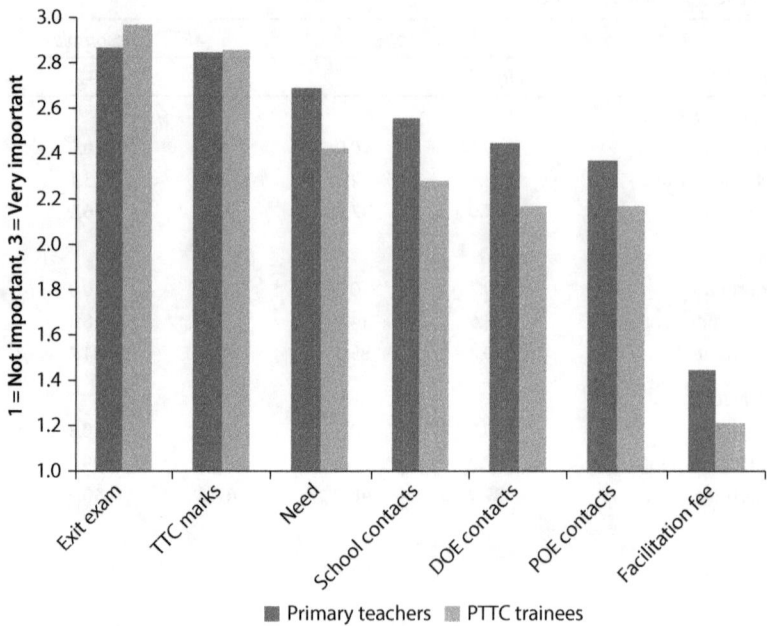

Source: World Bank 2012a, 2012b.
Note: DOE = District Office of Education; POE = Provincial Office of Education; PTTC = provincial teacher training center; TTC = teacher training center.

are not much more positive—only 36 percent say they would consider it. The most common reason is the distance ("too far"), followed by "very difficult" and "not enough pay." The responses highlight the importance of being near family networks and suggest that more local recruitment could be useful.

Only about 14 percent of teachers stated they would consider working in a remote area (table 3.3). Not surprisingly, their main reasons are distance and salary. Indeed, when asked what would persuade them to consider teaching in a remote area, the most common response was a "larger pay incentive." A sizeable group stated that in-kind payments might convince them to consider a remote posting.

To stimulate teacher interest in working in hard-to-staff remote and/or disadvantaged areas, the Cambodian government has implemented a bonus pay scheme (see table 4.7). But only about half of TTC trainees and about 60 percent of teachers have heard of it (see tables 3.2 and 3.3). Only a very small percentage of trainees willing to consider a remote placement (18 percent in RTTCs, 5.4 percent in PTTCs) cited the bonus as the reason. Trainees who have heard of the bonus thought its value was extremely small, between 59,000 riel (PTTC) and 85,000 riel (RTTC). So the placement bonus has not raised interest in teaching in remote schools.

Roughly 84 percent of teachers working in remote areas indicated that they receive the monthly pay bonus, though many payments are severely delayed (by about 71 days on average). The actual amount reported by teachers—averaging

Table 3.2 Trainees on Working in Remote Areas
Percent, unless otherwise indicated

Variable	Full samples		PTTC subsamples		
	RTTC	PTTC	12+2	9+2	Remote
Would you consider working in remote school?					
Yes (percent)	18.6	**33.0+**	30.0	37.7	35.7
If no, why not?					
Too far away	49.0	58.6	55.1	64.6	65.8
Very difficult	24.5	19.4	20.7	17.2	14.8
Not enough pay	21.6	19.2	22.1	14.2	16.9
Other	4.9	2.9	2.2	4.0	2.6
If yes, why?					
Extra pay incentive	17.9	5.4	5.3	5.5	6.1
Teachers are needed	55.4	44.3	42.6	46.3	40.0
I am from remote	7.1	35.2	37.1	32.8	43.0
Other	19.6	15.2	15.0	15.4	11.0
Are you aware of the bonus pay incentive for working in remote school?					
Yes	50.8	51.2	63.6	**32.0***	48.4
If yes, how much do you think it is worth? (thousands of riel)	85.4	59.4	54.5	78.4	66.2
Sample size (number)	301	651	387	264	257

Source: World Bank 2012b.
Note: PTTC = provincial teacher training center; RTTC = regional teacher training center. All results are based on weighted data. Tests of significance are used to compare RTTC and PTTC averages (significant differences highlighted in PTTC column), 12+2 and 9+2 averages (significant differences highlighted in 9+2 column), and remote and nonremote PTTC averages (highlighted in remote column).
* = Difference in average/percentage is significantly different at 0.05 level (two-tail); + = Difference in average/percentage is significantly different at 0.10 level. Boldface also used to highlight significant differences.

Table 3.3 Teachers and Trainees on Working in Remote Areas
Percent, unless otherwise indicated

Variable	Trainee samples		Teacher samples	
	RTTC	PTTC	all	remote
Are you aware of the bonus pay incentive for working in remote school?				
Yes	50.8	51.2	59.9	—
If yes, how much do you think it is worth? (thousands of riel)	85.4	59.4	—	—
Would you consider working in remote school?				
Yes	18.6	33.0	14.4	—
If working in remote area, do you receive bonus?				
Yes	—	—	—	83.5
If yes, how much? (thousands of riel)	—	—	—	41.6
Sample size (number)	301	651	676	177

Source: World Bank 2012a, 2012b.
Note: PTTC = provincial teacher training center; RTTC = regional teacher training center. All results are based on weighted data. — = question not applicable to sample.

about 40,000 riel a month, or $10—is substantially lower than what trainees reported, suggesting a mismatch between expectation and reality. Many felt a larger amount is needed.

Why are some trainees interested in remote positions? The most common reason was simply "teachers are needed." A small but significant proportion of PTTC (though not RTTC) trainees—about 10 percent—said they were interested because they are from remote areas.

These results have clear policy implications. First, the placement bonus is not well advertised within TTCs, limiting its recruiting potential. Second, the bonus is too small. Third, local recruitment may help staff remote schools.

Bibliography

World Bank. 2012a. Teacher Survey, World Bank, Washington, DC.

———. 2012b. Teacher Training College Survey, World Bank, Washington, DC.

CHAPTER 4

How Well Do Teachers Perform?

Key Messages

Several challenges face teacher quality in Cambodia. First, incentives do little to motivate top performance or to raise student achievement. Many teachers are unaware of bonuses for remote/disadvantaged placement or are uninterested because of distance and salary limitations. Bonuses for good teaching are widely awarded, but there is no evidence that they relate to teacher—or student—performance. Hampering incentive policies are perceptions that the bonuses are small.

Second, the teacher evaluation system is disconnected from teacher performance, teacher competencies, or student learning. The current Ministry of Education, Youth, and Sport (MoEYS) teacher evaluation form, derived from the national civil servant evaluation form, assesses teachers on their merits as civil servants. If these evaluations are to motivate top performance and improve student learning outcomes, the form needs to be linked with the teacher standards.

Third, teacher support can be improved. On the surface, the support system has many positive features: regular technical meetings, director visits to classrooms, and teacher satisfaction with their profession. But a more dynamic and collaborative working environment is needed.

Fourth, external measures of teacher quality, such as classroom observations, underscore the need to move away from teacher-centered instruction to more effective pedagogical strategies. The lack of lesson plans and student-initiated questions is a concern. Class time could be used more efficiently, with less dead time.

Finally, much work remains in adapting teacher standards to the average classroom. Only about half of teachers have heard of the teacher standards, and about 25 percent have had them explained. Thirty percent of school directors have not heard of them, and only about half indicated that the standards play a substantial role in the school's work.

Teacher Performance

How do Cambodian teachers perform? To answer this question, the World Bank commissioned a teacher policy survey in 150 primary schools throughout the country, observed classroom instruction, and administered a mathematics and

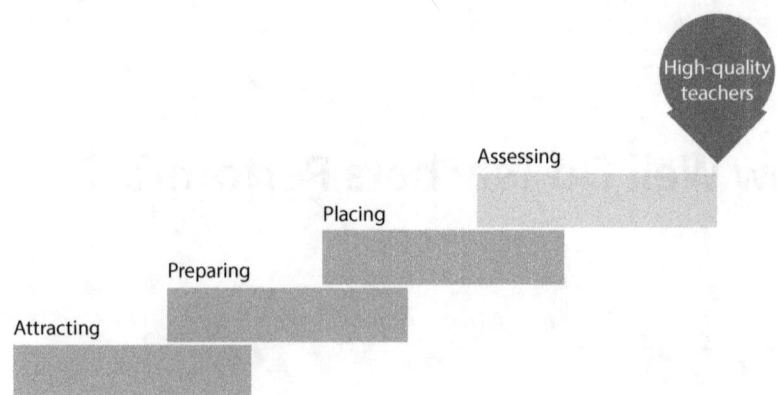

pedagogical content knowledge (PCK) assessment (see chapter 5). More than 680 teachers and school directors were interviewed. Their responses shed light on performance incentives, instruction quality, and teaching capacity. The analysis diagnoses teacher quality and management in Cambodian primary schools.

Several stark challenges emerge. First, incentives are not improving learning outcomes. Second, a less than interactive working environment does little to improve teaching quality. Third, evaluations bear little relation to teacher performance and competency. Fourth, much work remains in incorporating teacher standards in the average classroom. Incorporating the teacher standards can make teaching more student centric.

Incentives, Salaries, and Teacher Placement

How do incentives affect teacher performance, evaluations, and placement in Cambodia?

Cambodian teacher incentives are almost exclusively monetary. Teacher salaries have two components: the base salary and salary supplements. There are five categories of salary supplements: functional allowances; pedagogic allowances; placement/risk allowances; special work allowances for teachers covering multigrade, double-shift, and overtime teaching; and family-related allowances.

Base Salary

All teachers receive a base salary determined by grade and civil servant step schedule, which is composed of the product of the base salary index (table 4.1) and the annually revised unit indicator index (table 4.2). The base salary has increased by about 20 percent a year over the last decade.

Upper secondary school teachers start their careers at A3, equivalent to Provincial Office of Education (POE) and provincial teacher training center (PTTC)/regional teacher training center (RTTC) directors. Lower secondary school teachers start at B3, equivalent to POE deputy directors and/or District Office of Education (DOE) directors. Primary school teachers start at C3, as do

Table 4.1 Base Salary Index

Type	Level	Steps												
Grade		14	13	12	11	10	9	8	7	6	5	4	3	2	1
A	1									436	457	482	506	528	550
	2					361	373	387	402	419	437	454	467	478	487
	3	315	323	331	340	349	359	369	380	390	399	407	414	420	425
B	1									308	324	344	360	374	385
	2					252	262	272	283	295	306	316	325	333	340
	3	220	225	230	236	243	251	259	266	273	279	284	289	293	297
C	1									212	223	235	245	254	262
	2					173	178	785	193	201	208	215	222	228	233
	3	150	154	158	163	168	174	179	184	188	192	195	198	200	202
D	1									141	149	157	164	170	175
	2					113	117	122	128	134	139	144	148	152	155
	3	100	102	104	106	109	112	116	120	123	126	129	131	133	135

Sources: MoEYS 2013; Cambodia Administrative Reform General Secretariat 2010.
Note: Those who are C2–3 and D1–3 (gray area) will receive 320,000 riel of base salary regardless of their grades and steps from September 2013.

Table 4.2 Annual Unit Indicator for Base Salary

Year	Unit indicator per index
2004	345
2007	500
2009	720
2010	870
2011	1,050
2012	1,260
2013	1,520

Source: MoEYS 2013.

most preprimary teachers with preservice training. Few teachers are categorized at rank D (table 4.3). In August 2013, the government issued a subdecree setting the monthly minimum base salary of lower-level civil servants (D3 to C2 in table 4.1) at 320,000 riel ($80). This subdecree has been effective since September 1, 2013.

Functional Allowances

The functional allowance adds to the base salary of civil servants who have attained certain positions or worked a minimum threshold of years. Functional allowances are divided into five steps according to duration and work experience (table 4.4). All teachers receive functional allowances (table 4.5). Ministry officials have advocated for higher functional allowances for teachers than for other civil servants to signal their respect for teaching, recognizing that the work is difficult and that teachers lack clear pathways for promotion.[1]

Table 4.3 Positions in Each Grade

Grade	Teaching profession	Equivalent (approximate) positions of nonteaching staff and school directors
A1	Higher education and upper secondary school teachers (NIE graduates)	Rector, Director General, Inspector General
A2		Vice Rector, Dean, Deputy DG, Deputy Inspector General, Director of Department, Inspector of Inspectorate
A3		Vice Dean, Director of POE, Deputy Director of Department, Director of RTTC, PTTC, Director of Upper Secondary School
B1	Lower secondary school teachers (RTTC graduates)	Chief of Office, Deputy Director of POE
B2		Deputy Chief of Office (central), Chief of Office (provincial)
B3		Deputy Chief of Office (provincial), Chief of Office (district), Director of Preprimary, Primary, and Lower Secondary School
C1	Primary school & ECE teachers (PTTC graduates)	Deputy Chief of Office (district), Deputy Director of Preprimary and Primary School, Staff of Office (province and district)
C2		
C3		
D1	Those who did not attend TTC	
D2		
D3		

Source: MoEYS 2013.
Note: DG = director general; ECE = early childhood education; NIE = National Institute of Education; POE = Provincial Office of Education; PTTC = provincial teacher training center; RTTC = regional teacher training center; TTC = teacher training center.

Table 4.4 Functional Allowance

Level	Work experience (years)
1	More than 16
2	10–16
3	6–10
4	3–6
5	Fewer than 3

Source: Cambodia Administrative Reform General Secretariat 2010.

Table 4.5 Monthly Functional Allowance for the Education Sector

	Title	Level 5	4	3	2	1
1	Dean	80,000	84,000	88,200	92,600	97,200
2	Vice Dean	78,000	81,900	86,000	90,300	94,800
3	Professor of Higher Education	77,000	80,900	85,000	89,300	93,800
4	Director of National University of Management	76,000	79,800	83,800	88,000	92,400
5	Director of Polytechnic Institution	76,000	79,800	83,800	88,000	92,400
6	Director of National Institute for Polytechnic Training	76,000	79,800	83,800	88,000	92,400
7	University Lecturer	75,000	78,800	82,800	87,000	91,400
8	Vice Director of National University of Management	74,000	77,700	81,600	85,700	90,000
9	Vice Director of Polytechnic Institution	74,000	77,700	81,600	85,700	90,000
10	Vice Director of National Institute for Polytechnic Training	74,000	77,700	81,600	85,700	90,000
11	Lower Secondary School Inspector	74,000	77,700	81,600	85,700	90,000
12	Upper Secondary School Principal	73,000	76,700	80,500	84,500	88,700
13	Director of RTTC	73,000	76,700	80,500	84,500	88,700

table continues next page

Table 4.5 Monthly Functional Allowance for the Education Sector *(continued)*

	Title	Level 5	4	3	2	1
14	Director of PTTC	73,000	76,700	80,500	84,500	88,700
15	Director of Technical & Vocational Center	73,000	76,700	80,500	84,500	88,700
16	Director of Lower Secondary Technical School (2 yrs after G. 12)	73,000	76,700	80,500	84,500	88,700
17	Director of Physical Ed & Sport High School	73,000	76,700	80,500	84,500	88,700
18	Director of Preschool Teacher Training Center	73,000	76,700	80,500	84,500	88,700
19	Vice Upper Secondary School Principal	72,000	75,600	79,400	83,400	87,600
20	Vice Director of RTTC	72,000	75,600	79,400	83,400	87,600
21	Vice Director of PTTC	72,000	75,600	79,400	83,400	87,600
22	Vice Director of Technical & Vocational Center	72,000	75,600	79,400	83,400	87,600
23	Vice Director of Lower Secondary Technical School (2 yrs after G. 12)	72,000	75,600	79,400	83,400	87,600
24	Vice Director of Physical Ed & Sport High School	72,000	75,600	79,400	83,400	87,600
25	Vice Director of Preschool Teacher Training Center	72,000	75,600	79,400	83,400	87,600
26	Upper Secondary School Teacher	71,000	74,600	78,300	82,200	86,300
27	Primary Inspector	69,000	72,500	76,100	79,900	83,900
28	Lower Secondary School Principal	68,000	71,400	75,000	78,800	82,800
29	Director of Provincial Vocational Training	68,000	71,400	75,000	78,800	82,800
30	Vice Lower Secondary School Principal	67,000	70,400	73,900	77,600	81,500
31	Vice Director of Provincial Vocational Training	67,000	70,400	73,900	77,600	81,500
32	Lower Secondary School Teacher	66,000	69,300	72,800	76,500	80,300
33	Primary School Principal	64,000	67,200	70,600	74,100	77,800
34	Preschool Principal	64,000	67,200	70,600	74,100	77,800
35	Vice Primary School Principal	63,000	66,200	69,500	73,000	76,700
36	Vice Preschool Principal	63,000	66,200	69,500	73,000	76,700
37	Basic Education Teachers	62,000	65,100	68,400	71,800	75,400
38	Primary and Preprimary School Teacher	60,000	63,000	66,200	69,500	73,000

Source: MoEYS 2013.
Note: G. = grade; PTTC = provincial teacher training center; RTTC = regional teacher training center.

Pedagogic Allowances

Pedagogic allowances add to the monthly functional allowances of education civil servants who have received formal pedagogy training at a Teacher Training Center (TTC) or National Institute of Education. Under this criterion, 79 percent of surveyed teachers are eligible to receive pedagogic allowances, which are administered according to the civil servant categories (table 4.6).

Placement/Risk Allowance

Teachers in disadvantaged or remote areas receive placement/risk allowances each month to assist with health costs and other hardships of working in these locations (table 4.7).[2] These teachers also often get promoted faster. Seventy percent of teachers in nondisadvantaged or nonremote schools are promoted one step higher on the basic salary index (see table 4.1) about every two years if they perform satisfactorily. In contrast, 100 percent of teachers in disadvantaged districts or remote provinces are promoted regardless of their performance evaluations.

Table 4.6 Category for Pedagogic Allowance
Riel per month

Category	Allowance
A	12,000
B	10,000
C	8,000
D	6,000

Source: Cambodia Administrative Reform General Secretariat 2010.

Table 4.7 Placement Allowance
Riel per month

Area	Allowance
Disadvantaged area	40,000
Remote area (urban)	50,000
Remote area (rural)	60,000

Source: MoEYS 2013.

Table 4.8 Overtime Teaching at Secondary School
Riel per hour

Grade taught	Allowance
Upper secondary	9,300
Lower secondary	5,200
Lower secondary (by primary teacher)	2,000

Source: MoEYS 2013.

Special Work Incentives

There are several incentives for additional work, such as multigrade teaching (teaching more than one class at the same time), double-shift teaching (teaching both morning and afternoon classes), and overtime teaching (table 4.8). These strategies have been instituted to cope with teacher shortages in rural/remote areas. Multigrade teachers receive an additional 60 percent of their monthly salaries for teaching two grades and 80 percent for teaching three grades. Double-shift teachers receive an additional 100 percent, and teachers who attend monthly teacher meetings for technical/collaborative discussion receive some additional allowance.

Family-Related Allowances

The government offers some allowances for family conditions, including child allowances, spouse allowances, and maternity allowances.

Performance Incentives

Most teachers are aware of the good teaching performance award, and about 70 percent (more in urban areas) have received it (figure 4.1). The average award—about one-third of a monthly salary—is fairly small, suggesting it does little to attract people to teaching or motivate teachers to work harder (box 4.1).

What kind of teacher is most likely to receive the good teaching performance award? Given the award's prevalence, its receipt is unlikely to depend mainly on teaching ability. Teachers with more education are marginally more likely to receive it, head teachers significantly more likely, and contract teachers much less likely (table 4.9). But most indicators are insignificant. There is no evidence that teachers with more mathematics knowledge (content or teaching) are more likely to receive the award. School characteristics do not significantly affect award rates, suggesting fairly even selection across schools.

Many teachers receive the double-shift allowance, but very few receive extra pay for multigrade teaching or overtime. About 19 percent of teachers (27 percent of rural teachers, 39 percent of remote teachers, and less than 3 percent of urban teachers) reported working a double shift, and all but a very small percentage of these reported receiving the double-shift allowance. The double-shift pay bonus is a little more than one month's average pay. The teachers reported an average annual salary increase of roughly 470,000 riel, or about $118. The average delay in receiving this bonus was more than 50 days. But 77 percent of double-shift teachers (91 percent of remote teachers) indicated they were satisfied with the bonus.

Double-shift teachers reported favorable impressions of their work situations. Most of these teachers feel that they have enough time to prepare all their classes and can provide equal quality in each class (figure 4.2).

Figure 4.1 Has Teacher Heard of or Received Good Performance Award?

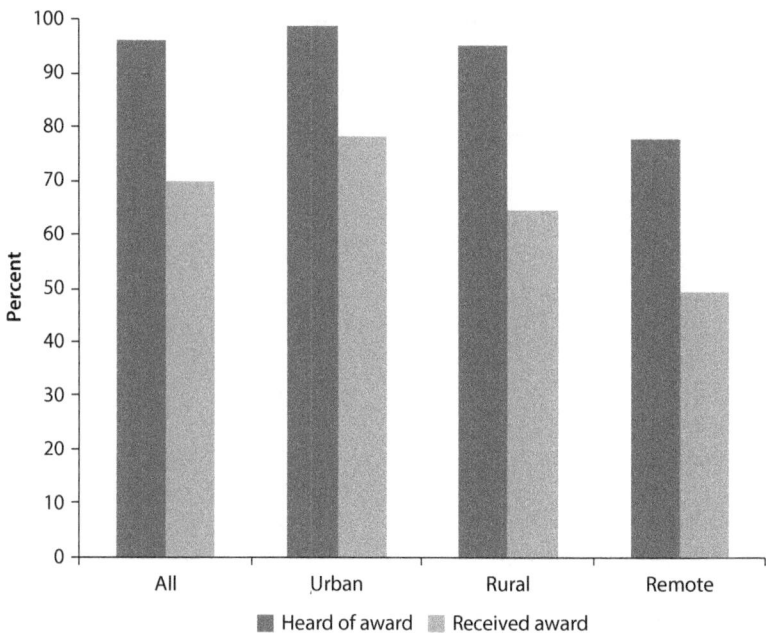

Source: World Bank 2012a.

Box 4.1 How Incentives Combine to Produce Total Teacher Compensation

Table B4.1.1 illustrates how incentives combine to produce total teacher remuneration. This calculation presents minimum income for new teachers at each educational level according to the following conditions: working in an average school (that is, nondisadvantaged and nonremote) with no overtime, multigrade, or double-shift teaching and no special family-related allowances.

Table B.4.1.1 New Teacher Minimum Income with Incentives

Teaching level	Basic salary index	Basic salary (riel)	Functional allowance	Pedagogic allowance	Other incomes	Total amount
Primary	C3/14 (with former salary scale)	150 x 1520 = 228,000	60,000	8,000	0	296,000 KHR (US$74)
Primary	C3/14 (with updated salary scale from Sep/13)	320,000 (minimum rate*)	60,000	8,000	0	388,000 KHR (US$97)
Lower secondary	B3/14 (no revision in 2013)	220 x 1520 = 334,400	66,000	10,000	0	410,400 KHR (US$102.6)
Upper secondary	C3/14 (no revision in 2013)	315 x 1520 = 478,800	71,000	12,000	0	561,800 KHR (US$140.5)

Note: * = Minimum rate for pre-primary and primary teachers from September 2013.

Table 4.9 Covariates of Teacher Receiving Good Teaching Performance Award
Probit

Variable	Coefficient	t-statistic
Teacher is male	−0.13	0.94
Teacher years of education	0.09	1.69*
Teacher experience	0.03	1.31
Teacher experience at this school	0.03	1.27
Teacher has other job	−0.06	0.39
Teacher number of grades	0.04	0.27
Teacher grade taught[a]		
Grade 2	−0.14	0.51
Grade 3	−0.17	0.68
Grade 4	−0.15	0.69
Grade 5	−0.29	1.24
Grade 6	0.31	1.21
Type of teacher[b]		
Head teacher	0.57	2.36**
Contract teacher	−1.61	2.88***
Teacher PCK	−0.26	0.71
Teacher content knowledge	0.02	0.06
School size	0.001	1.30
School is rural	0.16	0.70

table continues next page

Table 4.9 Covariates of Teacher Receiving Good Teaching Performance Award
(continued)

Variable	Coefficient	t-statistic
School is remote	0.37	1.14
% parents with cell phone	0.28	1.07
Parents' average education	0.02	0.51
Sample size (number)	613	

Sources: Teacher Survey 2012; various databases.
Note: Probit model used for dichotomous dependent variable. Results are based on weighted data. See text for more detail.
a. Excluded category: grade 1.
b. Excluded category: full-time teacher.
Significance level: * = 0.10, ** = 0.05, *** = 0.01.

Other than for placement, school directors and TTC trainers reported almost no extra incentive pay.

Teacher incentives thus reward workload and placement rather than quality or performance. They do not significantly affect teacher pay. Due to its frequent granting and modest size, even the good teaching performance award hardly motivates teachers to do better.

Other Income Sources

Many teachers take on extra work with remedial classes, second jobs, and tutoring. About 97 percent of teachers report giving remedial classes, but almost all of these classes take place on Thursday—an inservice day—during the teacher's regular working hours. About 34 percent of teachers tutor students outside of class, presumably during the teacher's own private time, 13 percent more than in the last Public Expenditure Tracking Survey (Benveniste, Marshall, and Aranjo 2008). In rural areas, the average is 17 percent, in remote areas 10 percent, and in urban areas 55.4 percent, reflecting larger demand among urban families. On average, the teachers work with about 16 students, usually charging 300–500 riel an hour. This translates into an average monthly pay of about 280,000 riel, a sizeable supplement to an average monthly salary.

Teaching grade and experience in a particular school also contribute to the likelihood of tutoring (table 4.10). Teachers with more experience in the same school (rather than overall experience) are more likely to cultivate relationships with families or be seen as a respected figure. Older children are more likely to receive tutoring.

MoEYS has officially outlawed private tutoring. Although the government tried in 2005 to prohibit unofficial fees from activities such as purchasing exam papers from teachers and in 2008 labeled private tutoring unethical, school administrators have not enforced these policies. Private tutoring has actually expanded and is distorting the mainstream curricula by shifting content from regular classes to private tutorials (Brehm, Silova, and Mono 2012), so tutoring may actually be underreported in our teacher survey. The practice allows teachers to augment their salaries and provides extra class time for interested students.

Figure 4.2 Double-Shift Teacher Opinions on Quality

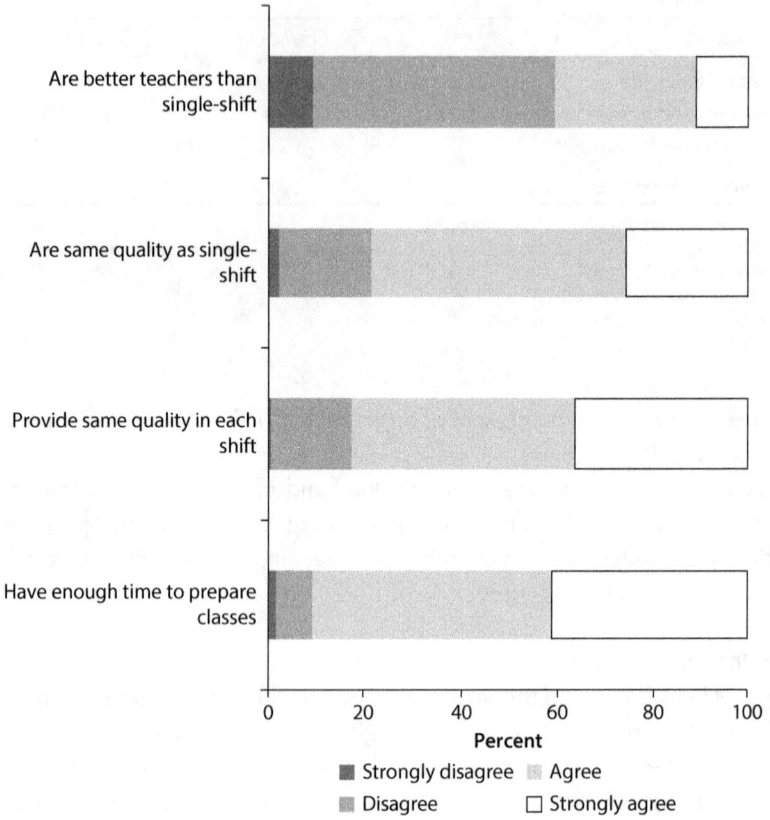

[Bar chart showing percentages for four statements:
- Are better teachers than single-shift
- Are same quality as single-shift
- Provide same quality in each shift
- Have enough time to prepare classes

Legend: Strongly disagree, Disagree, Agree, Strongly agree]

Source: World Bank 2012a.

Table 4.10 Covariates of Tutoring
Probit

Variable	Coefficient	t-statistic
Teacher is male	−0.31	1.67*
Teacher years of education	0.04	0.70
Teacher experience	0.002	0.06
Teacher experience—this school	0.09	4.55***
Teacher salary level	−0.01	0.61
Teacher has other job	−0.79	4.17***
Teacher has double-shift bonus	−0.22	0.75
Teacher has remote school bonus	0.11	0.55
Number of grades taught	−0.17	0.45
School size	0.001	0.45
School is rural	−0.49	1.12
School is remote	−0.01	0.03

table continues next page

Table 4.10 Covariates of Tutoring *(continued)*

Variable	Coefficient	t-statistic
Grade taught		
Grade 2	0.61	1.34
Grade 3	1.17	3.40***
Grade 4	1.31	3.80***
Grade 5	1.31	3.37***
Grade 6	1.79	4.38***
Parents with cell phone	0.87	1.82*
Parents average education	0.03	0.46
Committee training average	0.55	0.91
Committee meetings	0.90	1.12
Committee influence average	−0.61	1.72*
Sample size (number)		578

Sources: World Bank 2012a; various databases.
Note: Probit model used for dichotomous dependent variable. Results are based on weighted data.
1 = teacher reports tutoring income, 0 = does not report tutoring income.
Significance level: * = 0.10, ** = 0.05, *** = 0.01.

But not all teachers will have access to students who can pay the extra fees, and teachers may restrict tutoring to students who can pay—or those who can pay the most.

Cambodian teachers are more likely than other civil servants to have other jobs, despite recent salary increases (table 4.11). Nearly half of primary school teachers, mostly in rural and remote areas, report a second job, usually farming in rural areas or small-item vending in urban ones. Second jobs take up an average of about 14 hours a week at about 150,000 riel, although in remote areas the pay is much lower.

Teachers are thus spending a substantial amount of time in second jobs and receiving sizeable income supplements from them. Some teachers earn more income from their second jobs than from their teaching jobs. The frequency of second jobs may result from inadequate teacher pay—teachers have to work extra hours to support themselves and their families. Surveyed teachers welcomed the recent salary increases primarily for this reason.

Teacher Support, Evaluation, and Satisfaction

Teacher Interactions

An ideal teaching environment has multiple informative interactions among teachers and between teachers and school directors and other support personnel. It is encouraging that 98 percent of the sampled primary teachers (just under 90 percent in remote schools) report having technical meetings that they regularly attend. The main topics discussed include teaching methodology, lesson planning, and how to improve student learning. Teachers considered the meetings "very useful" (71 percent) or "useful" (28 percent). The most commonly

Table 4.11 Teacher Second Jobs
Percent, unless otherwise indicated

		By location		
Variable	All teachers	Urban	Rural	Remote
Do you currently have another job?	48.1	**24.6***	**66.6***	**69.2***
If yes, in what sector?				
Farming	66.9	24.9	78.3	86.2
Small item vendor	19.2	45.2	12.2	6.2
Motor driver	4.0	9.4	2.5	2.8
Other	19.9	20.5	7.0	4.8
How many hours a week do you spend in this activity?	14.4	**18.8***	**12.3***	17.0
How much do you earn a week in this activity? (thousands of riel)	151.6	134.0	165.4	**70.9***
Sample size (number)	677	138	478	52

Source: World Bank 2012a.
Note: Results are based on weighted data.
* = Category mean is significantly different from average at 0.05 level.

requested changes were to bring in outside trainers, hold the meetings more frequently, exchange more experiences among teachers, and have all teachers participate, suggesting that at least some teachers would like a more dynamic training environment. Technical meetings are a standard feature of primary schools, and teachers are satisfied with their impact.

But there is room to encourage more teacher–teacher interaction. Teachers, on average, frequently discuss teaching, but only about 10 percent do so daily (figure 4.3). Visits to other classrooms are much more limited: more than 60 percent of teachers report never visiting another teacher's classroom to observe his/her teaching, even though most schools (except in rural and remote areas) have systems for teachers to observe other teachers (figure 4.4).

Despite limited interaction among teachers, there is frequent and useful interaction between teachers and school directors. In most schools (67.1 percent), the director visits the teacher's classroom at least once a month—in remote schools even more often (table 4.12). In many schools, the visits are much less frequent (every 3–6 months), but very few teachers report never being visited by their directors. More than 80 percent of teachers receive "a lot of" or "some" feedback from directors based on these visits. A similar percentage of teachers report finding the feedback either "very helpful" (28 percent) or "helpful" (48 percent).

DOE personnel make far fewer visits to the teacher's classrooms than directors. On average, DOE officials visit about twice a year. Many teachers, especially in remote schools, report never being visited in their classroom by DOE personnel. POE officials visit even less frequently.

Schools have regular technical meetings, some teacher–teacher interaction, and semiregular classroom visits. TTC trainers report similar features (see chapter 2), although primary school teachers report more classroom observations by directors.

Figure 4.3 Teacher–Teacher Interactions

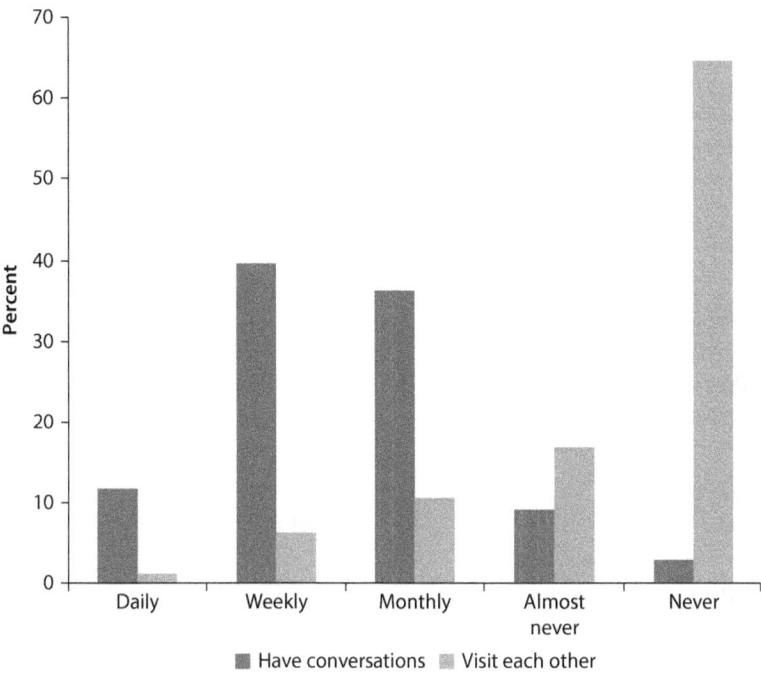

Source: World Bank 2012a.

Figure 4.4 Does School Have System for Teachers to Observe Other Teachers?

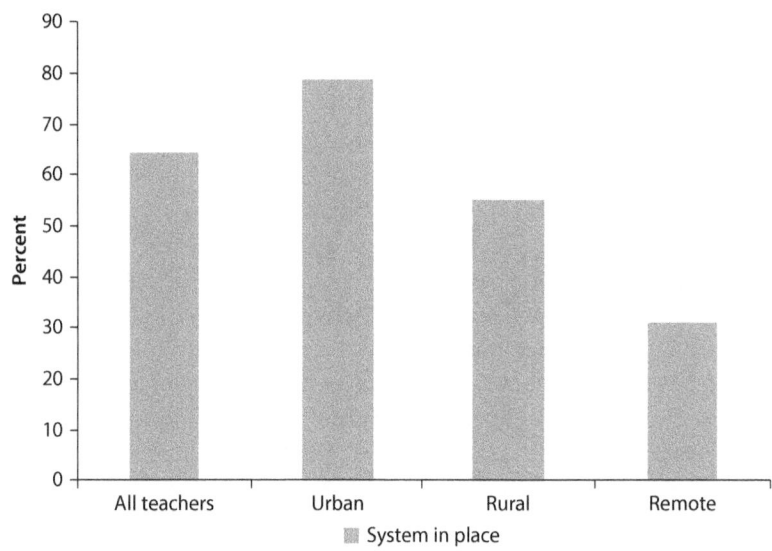

Source: World Bank 2012a.

Table 4.12 Teacher Observations by Director and DOE Staff
Percent, unless otherwise indicated

Variable	All teachers	By location		
		Urban	Rural	Remote
Observed by director				
At least once/month	67.1	65.7	67.4	81.2
Every three months	11.6	9.7	13.6	6.7
Twice a year	11.6	13.6	10.2	5.2
Once a year	3.5	5.4	2.1	2.1
Never	6.1	5.5	6.7	4.8
How much feedback does director give?				
A lot of feedback	33.3	39.0	29.7	20.9
Some feedback	47.9	42.3	51.7	57.8
Little feedback	16.3	16.7	15.7	18.8
No feedback	2.5	2.1	2.9	2.5
Observed by DOE staff				
At least once/month	11.4	5.9	16.0	11.8
Every three months	26.2	27.3	25.4	23.5
Twice a year	23.3	22.1	25.0	15.0
Once a year	19.4	26.2	14.0	15.5
Never	19.8	18.6	19.7	34.3
Sample size (number)	677	138	478	52

Source: World Bank 2012a.
Note: DOE = District Office of Education. All numbers are frequencies that sum to 100 within variable. Results are based on weighted data.

But we cannot conclude from these responses that primary schools have dynamic or robust teacher support systems. Without data on the content of these interactions, it is difficult to assess how much they improve teachers' work in the classroom.

Teacher Evaluation

MoEYS prioritizes evaluating teachers and has built a system to conduct teacher evaluations nationwide. Most teachers (about 77 percent) "strongly agree" that the most hard-working and effective teachers receive the best evaluations (figure 4.5); less than 4 percent disagree.

About 80 percent of teachers are familiar with the official evaluation format, and more than 70 percent report being evaluated with it (figure 4.6). But these standardized evaluation practices have not reached all areas: rural and remote teachers are much less likely to be familiar with the form or be evaluated with it. On average, most teachers are evaluated using this form every one or two years (figure 4.7). A small percentage of teachers reports being evaluated more than once a year, and a significant percentage—mostly in remote areas—have never been evaluated.

Some schools do not use the MoEYS teacher evaluation form, so evaluation needs to be standardized. More than half of teachers who were not evaluated

Figure 4.5 Do You Agree that Hard-Working Teachers Receive the Best Teacher Evaluations?

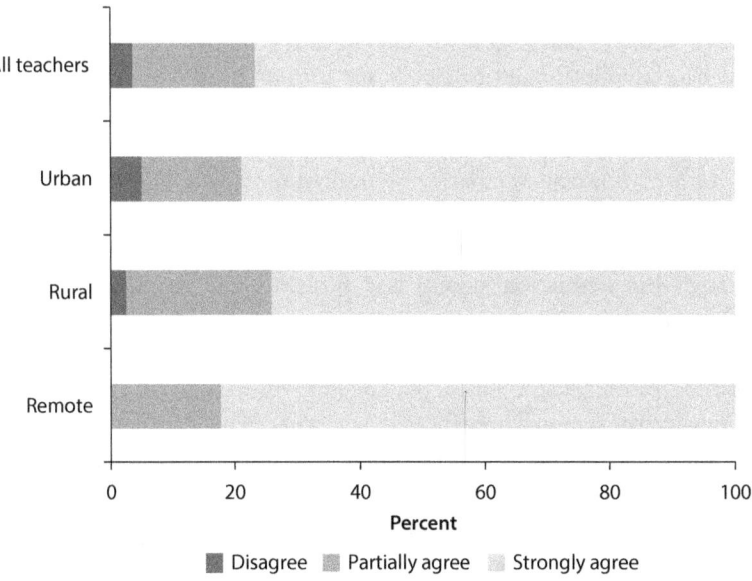

Source: World Bank 2012a.

Figure 4.6 Is Teacher Familiar with DoP Evaluation Form, and Have They Been Evaluated with Form?

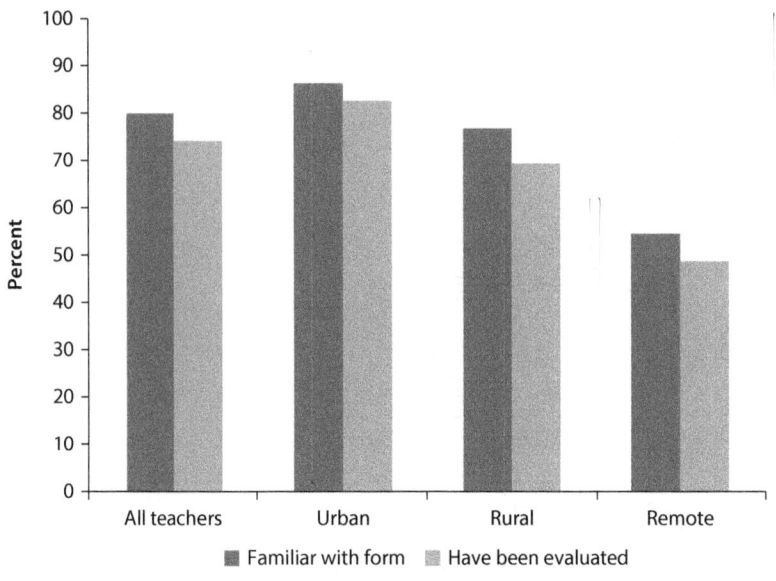

Source: World Bank 2012a.
Note: DoP = Department of Planning.

with the common civil servant format were evaluated with some other format; 13 percent were not evaluated at all.

Although 75 percent of teachers are aware of teaching evaluations, many lack knowledge of the details (figure 4.8). Most of the 85 percent of surveyed teachers who had been evaluated had only a "little" or "some" knowledge about the evaluation process. Few teachers were "very knowledgeable" about it. Teachers have little idea how to prepare, what will be asked, or how they can improve. Sharing information and standardizing evaluation would help teachers develop the skills they will be evaluated on and improve evaluation quality, transparency, and sustainability.

Although the evaluation system is a positive step, its effectiveness is constrained: its assessment of teachers as civil servants has little to do with teacher performance, teacher competencies, or student learning. The MoEYS teacher evaluation form reflects the values the government requires of civil servants, such as "working for the national benefit" and "solidarity." The form's four questions rate teachers on a scale of 1–20 on how much they display: (a) "initiative and result orientation;" (b) "professional ethics, responsibility, and work discipline;" (c) efforts to take "into account the national benefit;" and (d) "solidarity, moral, and social activities." There are no formal scoring guidelines. The evaluation form and guidelines thus need to be revised in line with the teacher standards if they are to

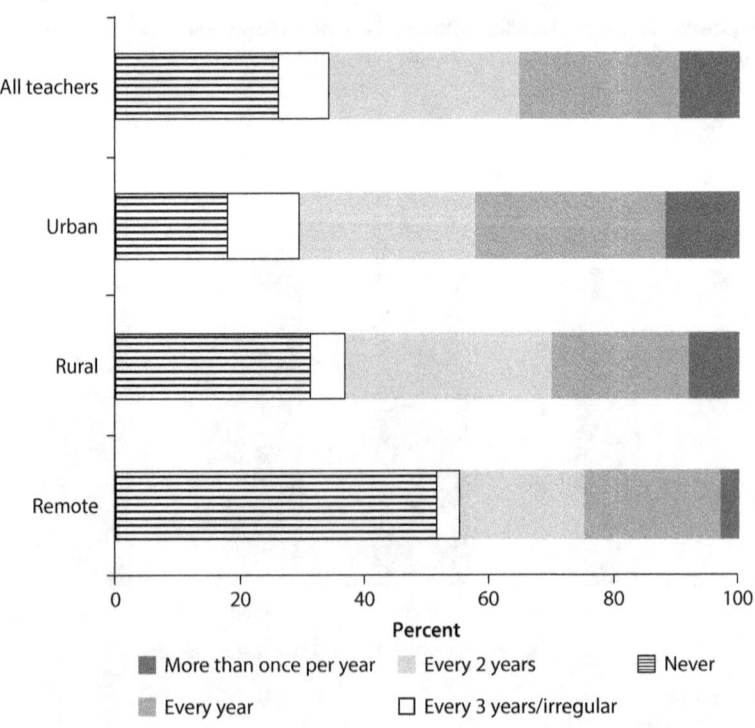

Figure 4.7 Frequency of Teacher Evaluations using DoP Form

Source: World Bank 2012a.
Note: DoP = Department of Planning.

Figure 4.8 How Knowledgeable Is Teacher about the Evaluation System?

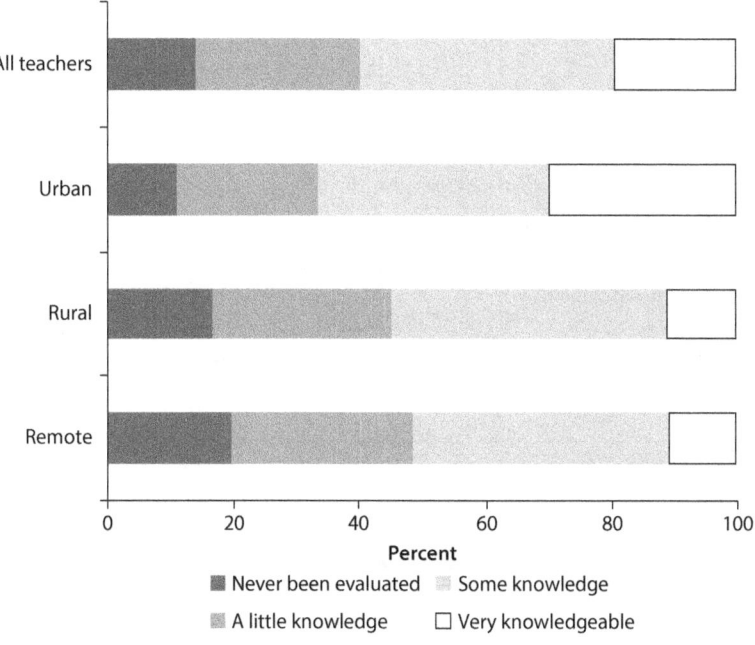

Source: World Bank 2012a.

motivate top performance and improve student learning outcomes. Thirty percent of directors—even more in rural and remote schools—have not even heard of the teacher standards (table 4.13). Most directors who are familiar with the teacher standards report that the standards have "a lot" of influence on the school's work.

Teachers thus work in minimally supportive environments with marginal interaction or enriching training, but they do have regular technical meetings and receive director feedback from classroom visits. Most teachers are familiar with teacher evaluations and feel they are fair. However, the evaluation form itself has little to do with teaching and learning outcomes and does little to improve them.

School Director Behavior and Perceptions

School director behavior and perceptions can shed additional light on incentives and teacher evaluation and support. The information provided by school directors is largely consistent with other sources.

Many school directors are unaware of the remote area teaching bonus, and very few would consider working in a remote school (table 4.14). Almost all of the remote school directors report receiving their bonuses, although they also report payment delays and dissatisfaction with the bonus amount. For directors who are not interested in working in remote areas, the most frequently cited reason to do so is a larger placement bonus.

Table 4.13 Director Knowledge of Teacher Standards
Percent, unless otherwise indicated

	Directors	
Variable	Whole sample	Rural/remote
Have you heard of the teacher standards?		
Yes	70.0	66.4
Have the teacher standards been explained to you?		
Yes	51.6	51.7
Describe the influence of the teacher standards on your own work.		
Have not heard of them	30.0	33.6
No influence	2.6	4.4
A little influence	14.2	15.5
A lot of influence on my work	53.2	46.5
Sample size (number)	149	121

Source: World Bank 2012b.
Note: All results are based on weighted data.

Table 4.14 Working in Remote Areas and Placement Bonus

	Directors	
Variable	Whole sample	Rural/remote
Are you aware of the bonus pay incentive for working in remote school?		
Yes	42.6	44.5
If yes, how much do you think it is worth? (standard deviation)	603,115 (91,887)	610,580 (146,402)
Would you consider working in remote school?		
Yes	15.2	n.a.
If working in remote area, do you receive bonus?		
Yes	n.a.	86.3
If yes, how much? (thousands of riel)	n.a.	42,880 (1,513)
Have there been delays in payment?	n.a.	83.2
Are you satisfied with the bonus?	n.a.	46.2
Sample size	149	121

Source: TTC World Bank 2012b.
Note: All results are based on weighted data; standard deviations in parentheses. There is some disagreement between number of schools classified as remote and director reports on whether or not they are assigned to a remote school; n.a. = not applicable.

School management participation usually includes the director and deputy director, with less participation from teachers, school committee members, parents, and community members (table 4.15). Meetings usually happen every quarter or month. Director responses do not differ significantly between rural or remote schools and the sample averages.

Encouragingly, almost every school director reports having a school support committee (SSC), and most SSCs include (at least) the director, parents, and community members. Most directors indicate that these committees contribute

Table 4.15 School Management Team According to Director
Percent, unless otherwise indicated

Variable	Directors Whole sample	Directors Rural/remote
Have management team in place?		
Yes	86.5	85.0
Who is on team?		
Principal	97.8	96.2
Deputy principal	87.7	80.7
Other administrator	72.0	63.4
Teacher	68.7	74.6
School committee member	54.5	61.6
Parents	30.7	32.9
Community members	32.7	30.0
Average size of team	63.5	62.8
How often has team met this year?		
No team in place	13.5	15.0
Never	3.2	4.4
Once	0.9	1.4
Every semester	14.0	12.9
Quarterly	27.0	27.8
Monthly	32.6	36.1
Weekly	5.7	0
Sample size (number)	149	121

Source: TTC World Bank 2012b.
Note: All results are based on weighted data. For team members results are percentages that indicated "yes"; for team meetings the results are frequencies that sum to 100.0 (or close).

substantially to school decisions (figure 4.9). Between 80 percent and 100 percent of directors affirmed that SSCs "make final decisions," "raise money," and "approve school budgets."

Unlike teachers, school directors have some interaction with district and/or provincial officials. Almost all agree that the DOE provides useful support and professional development, and understands individual school needs (table 4.16). Directors in all areas report meeting with DOE personnel about once every month and receiving fairly regular visits from DOE personnel—in some cases every six months but on average every three months or more often (table 4.17). In the context of teacher responses, these responses suggest that DOE personnel rarely observe classrooms or meet with teachers on their school visits. The POE and Inspectorate General (IG) visit less frequently—more than one-third of school directors indicate they do not receive IG visits.

School directors feel that their professional development could be strengthened (figure 4.10). Between 25 percent and 40 percent of directors report having received training in the current school year in the various professional

Figure 4.9 School Support Committee Roles According to Directors

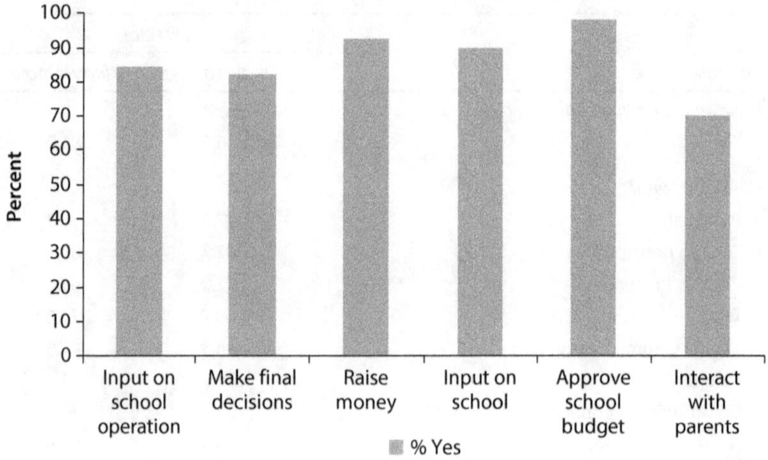

[Bar chart showing % Yes responses:
- Input on school operation: ~85
- Make final decisions: ~82
- Raise money: ~93
- Input on school: ~90
- Approve school budget: ~98
- Interact with parents: ~70]

Source: TTC World Bank 2012b.

Table 4.16 DOE Support According to School Directors
Percent, unless otherwise indicated

Variable	Directors Whole sample	Rural/remote
Do you agree with the following statements about DOE support?		
Provides sufficient instructional support to teachers in my school	90.6	88.5
Provides high-quality professional development to teachers in my school	89.6	84.5
Understands the particular needs of your school	87.8	85.5
Produces policy directives and official guidelines that change frequently	89.6	88.7
Provides me with useful feedback on performance	97.1	96.4
Since the beginning of this school year (2012–13), how many times have you attended meetings with DOE personnel?	6.5	5.6
Sample size (number)	149	121

Source: TTC World Bank 2012b.
Note: DOE = District Office of Education. All results are based on weighted data. In top part, all numbers refer to percentages.

development areas, particularly in curriculum and work plan development. Relatively little teacher evaluation training was given.

But director evaluation with the official Department of Planning (DoP) director evaluation form occurs fairly infrequently, according to school directors (table 4.18). Almost all of the school directors are familiar with this form, and about 55 percent indicated that they were evaluated with it every two years. Only about one-quarter of school directors report annual (or more frequent) formal evaluations (table 4.18).

Directors on average do not have substantial knowledge about the evaluation process, and only about half report having results explained to them (table 4.18).

Figure 4.10 Director Professional Development

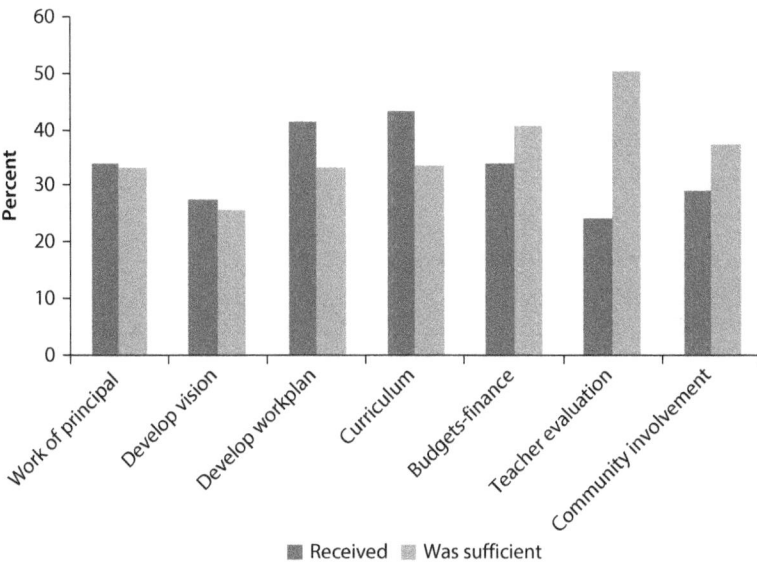

Source: TTC World Bank 2012b.

Table 4.17 School Director Evaluation
Percent, unless otherwise indicated

	Directors	
Variable	Whole sample	Rural/remote
How often does DOE supervise your work?		
Never	2.9	0.4
Once per year	4.1	3.4
Every six months	24.6	20.9
Every three months	44.8	41.2
Every month	23.7	34.2*
How helpful is the DOE feedback?		
Not very helpful	10.8	7.2
Helpful	58.5	63.6
Very helpful	30.7	29.1
How often does POE supervise your work?		
Never	15.7	11.5
Once per year	33.4	24.3
Every six months	33.9	43.6
Every three months	11.8	15.3
Every month	4.8	4.5*
How helpful is the POE feedback?		
Not very helpful	3.0	3.0
Helpful	66.2	67.5
Very helpful	30.8	29.5

table continues next page

Table 4.17 School Director Evaluation *(continued)*

Variable	Directors	
	Whole sample	Rural/remote
Never	34.0	30.8
Once per year	47.3	50.9
Every six months	12.4	11.1
Every three months	1.4	2.4
Every month	3.2	1.8
How helpful is the Inspectorate feedback?		
Not very helpful	3.0	6.0
Helpful	63.7	63.5
Very helpful	33.3	30.5
Sample size (number)	149	121

Source: TTC World Bank 2012b.
Note: DOE = District Office of Education; POE = Provincial Office of Education. All results are based on weighted data. All numbers are frequencies that sum to 100 percent (or close).
* = Overall frequencies for rural/remote schools are significantly different from those for urban schools.

This is particularly concerning since informative and useful feedback is an important part of evaluation.

But directors are fairly well informed about teacher evaluations and evaluate teachers often (table 4.19). About 85 percent of directors have also received training in using the teacher evaluation form. Directors report fairly regular teacher evaluations (table 4.20), many at least once a month (31.5 percent) or every three months (23.7 percent). But only about one-quarter of directors indicated that they give their teachers written evaluation summaries.

What actions do school directors take when teachers do not perform at an expected level? The most common response (about 50 percent) is to assign mentor teachers (table 4.20). This is followed by providing written notification (24.2 percent) and ordering more training (16.9 percent). In very few instances does the director report teachers to the DOE/POE or fire them.

School directors also raised concerns about lesson preparation and double-shift teaching. Most stated that their teachers' lessons are "pretty well prepared," but less than 1 percent said they are "well prepared" (table 4.21). School directors were also more likely to state that their teachers are "moderately prepared" to deliver high-quality education (53.6 percent) than "very prepared" (44.1 percent). And just over half of directors (54 percent) indicated that they had enough teachers in their schools. These challenges are more pronounced in rural and remote areas.

Unlike multigrade teaching, which is not widely used, double-shift teaching is found in 23 percent of schools and in about 35 percent of rural/remote schools. About 60 percent of directors feel that double-shift teachers provide the same quality as teachers who work only one shift, although a substantial proportion (about 38 percent) feel that quality is higher when the teacher only works one shift. Most school directors (almost 80 percent) feel the pay incentive for double-shift teachers is not sufficient.

Table 4.18 Director Experience with DoP Form
Percent, unless otherwise indicated

	Directors	
Variable	Whole sample	Rural/remote
Are you familiar with DoP director evaluation form?		
Yes	92.1	88.8
How often have you been evaluated?		
Never/not familiar	10.7	15.4
Not regularly	6.8	0.6
Every two school years	55.7	60.4
Once per school year	20.5	18.2
More than once per school year	5.6	4.5
Have the results of the evaluation even been explained to you?		
Yes	52.0	56.0
How would you rate your understanding of the evaluation framework?		
Not familiar	10.7	15.4
Little knowledge	4.2	5.7
Some knowledge	33.5	42.7
Very knowledgeable	51.6	36.3*
Do you agree that directors that work hard and are better prepared receive better evaluations?		
Strongly disagree	4.5	4.1
Partially agree	15.0	24.0
Strongly agree	80.5	71.9*
Sample size (number)	149	121

Source: TTC World Bank 2012b.
Note: DoP = Department of Planning. All results are based on weighted data. Knowledge and familiarity question numbers refer to percentages that indicated "yes." All other numbers are frequencies that sum to 100 per cent (or close).
* = Overall frequencies for rural/remote schools are significantly different from those for urban schools.

Table 4.19 Director Use of DoP Teacher Evaluation Form
Percent, unless otherwise indicated

	Directors	
Variable	Whole sample	Rural/remote
Are you familiar with DoP teacher evaluation form?		
Yes	89.3	84.0
Have you ever used this form in your school?		
Yes	85.0	76.9*
How would you rate your understanding of the teacher evaluation framework?		
Not familiar	15.0	23.1
Little knowledge	1.5	1.2
Some knowledge	13.9	20.9
Very knowledgeable	69.7	54.8*
Yes	86.1	81.7

table continues next page

Table 4.19 Director Use of DoP Teacher Evaluation Form *(continued)*

	Directors	
Variable	Whole sample	Rural/remote
Have you ever used a different form to evaluate teachers?		
Yes	35.9	32.4
Sample size (number)	149	121

Source: TTC World Bank 2012b.
Note: DoP = Department of Planning. All results are based on weighted data. All numbers refer to percentage who indicated yes, expect for understanding of teacher evaluation framework (frequencies).
* = Overall frequencies for rural/remote schools, or percentages (0–100%), are significantly different from those for urban schools.

Table 4.20 Director Teacher Evaluation and Support

	Directors	
Variable	Whole sample	Rural/remote
How often do you evaluate each teacher in your school?		
Never	1.7	2.8
Once per year	14.9	8.3
Every six months	26.7	21.5
Every three months	23.7	27.4
At least once per month	31.5	37.3
Do you provide a written summary of the evaluation?		
Yes	25.6	25.3
How often do you provide teachers with pedagogical support or advice in the classroom?		
Never	2.3	3.9
Occasionally	9.9	13.8
Regularly	71.4	71.1
Frequently	16.3	11.3
During last two years, have you taken following measures for underperforming teachers?		
Gave them written notification	24.2	15.0*
Sent them for more training	16.9	20.6
Assigned a teacher mentor	53.2	42.1*
Reported to POE/DOE	1.6	1.6
Fired the teacher	3.3	0*
Sample size (number)	149	121

Source: TTC World Bank 2012b.
Note: DOE = District Office of Education; POE = Provincial Office of Education. All results are based on weighted data. Numbers for first two questions are frequencies that sum to 100 percent (or close). For measures the questions refer to percentages that indicated yes.
* = Mean for rural/remote schools is significantly different from those for urban schools.

Quality Indicators: Teacher Capacity, Teaching Methodology, and Student Attendance

Classroom Teaching

We observed 286 classrooms using the same format as in chapter 2. Most of the classes were fourth grade.

Table 4.21 Director Appraisal of Teacher Quality and Incentives
Percent, unless otherwise indicated

	Directors	
Variable	Whole sample	Rural/remote
How well do teachers prepare their lesson plans in your school?		
Not prepared at all	0.7	1.2
Partially prepared	36.2	54.5
Pretty well prepared	62.4	44.4
Well prepared	0.7	0*
How prepared is the teaching staff in this school to provide high quality?		
Not prepared	0.4	0.7
Minimally prepared	2.0	3.0
Moderately prepared	53.6	72.5
Very prepared	44.1	23.9*
Do you have enough teachers in this school?		
Yes	54.4	39.0*
What percentage of teachers are in multigrade classrooms?	1.2	1.8
Is the quality the same in these classrooms as others?		
Yes, it is the same	55.9	44.6
No, the quality is higher in the multigrade classroom	0	0
No, the quality is higher in the regular classroom	44.1	55.4
What percentage of teachers are double shift teachers?	23.0	34.8*
Is the quality the same in these classrooms as others?		
Yes, it is the same	60.4	60.6
No, the quality is higher in the multigrade classroom	1.0	1.1
No, the quality is higher in the regular classroom	38.6	38.3
Do you feel the salary incentive for double shift teachers is enough?		
Yes	22.6	22.7
Sample size (number)	149	121

Source: TTC World Bank 2012b.
Note: All results are based on weighted data. Questions are a mixture of yes/no and frequencies that sum to 100 percent (or close).
* = Overall frequencies (or means) for rural/remote schools are significantly different from those for urban schools.

Attendance and Lesson Plans

On average, teachers took attendance in 91.1 percent of the classrooms, and in another 6 percent teachers said they took attendance but did not have the attendance book (table 4.22). This average varies somewhat by school location—an attendance book was visible in only 79.5 percent of remote school classrooms.

Less than half of the classrooms had a written lesson plan. Urban schools had the highest percentage, 66.2 percent, compared with only about 35 percent in rural and remote classrooms. Although a written lesson plan does not guarantee quality, it may predict a better functioning session because it provides some structure to class activities.

Table 4.22 Attendance and Lesson Plan
Percent

Variable	All schools	By location		
		Urban	Rural	Remote
Does teacher take attendance?				
No	2.9	2.5	3.2	2.7
Yes, but not present	6.1	0.8	9.1	17.8
Yes, and is present	91.1	**96.7+**	**87.7+**	**79.5+**
Is the lesson plan written out?				
Yes	47.6	66.2	34.7	34.7

Source: World Bank 2012a.
Note: All results are based on weighted data. Boldfaced numbers are referred to in the text.
+ = Category mean is significantly different from average at 0.10 level.

Classroom Time Segments

On average, about 8 percent of observed class time was spent in class management or no instruction (table 4.23). Urban schools had more class management challenges, while rural and remote schools had more down time with no instruction. The large cumulative amount of time "lost" signals room for better and more efficient class management.

Most class time (43 percent) was spent on instruction activities, which were fairly evenly distributed between teachers giving instruction, students copying, and students reading. But troublingly, students in remote classrooms copied for almost 25 percent of the class time, much more than in other school locations. Quality in these schools may thus be low because students are less engaged with instruction.

Recitation activities—mostly teacher centric—took up about 20 percent of class time. For most of the recitation time, teachers asked students questions, rather than students asking questions of teachers (or receiving an answer). Students did not initiate much of the interaction.

The second largest block of time was devoted to work activities. On average, these activities—mostly individual seatwork—took up about 23 percent of the class. Little time was spent in discussions among students, group work, or kinesthetics.

The distribution of classroom activities varies little across the country (figure 4.11), with a few exceptions for individual activities such as copying and getting control of the class.

The class time segment observations, divided into three 20-minute periods, show that lessons adhere to an identifiable pattern (figure 4.12). Classes begin with some class management activities and then focus on teacher instruction. In the middle of the lesson, students devote more time to working on activities. But unlike the TTC classes, which end with less student work and more recitation and teacher involvement, the primary school classes end with students working. When students work through the end of class, the teacher may not have time to review the lesson and issue final comments. Primary school teachers also

How Well Do Teachers Perform?

Table 4.23 Class Time Use
Percentage of class time, unless otherwise indicated

Breakdown by activity	All schools	By location		
		Urban	Rural	Remote
Class management	8.1	9.2	7.6	5.5
Get control	5.5	8.1	3.9	1.8
No instruction	2.6	1.1	3.7	3.7
Instruction activities	43.3	37.8	46.5	54.9
Teacher instruction	14.0	11.8	15.4	17.5
Students copying	15.5	12.1	17.4	24.7
Students reading	13.8	13.9	13.7	12.7
Recitation	19.8	20.8	19.2	16.3
Question-answer	16.2	16.7	15.9	14.3
Student asking	0.5	0.4	0.6	0.1
Student receiving answer	3.1	3.7	2.7	1.9
Work activities	23.2	28.1	20.1	14.7
Seatwork	14.3	18.4	11.5	8.6
Discussion	3.9	4.1	3.9	2.7
Group work	4.3	4.9	4.0	3.2
Kinesthetics	0.7	0.7	0.7	0.2
Sample size (number)	284	55	202	26

Source: World Bank 2012a.
Note: All results are based on weighted data.

Figure 4.11 Time Segments by School Location

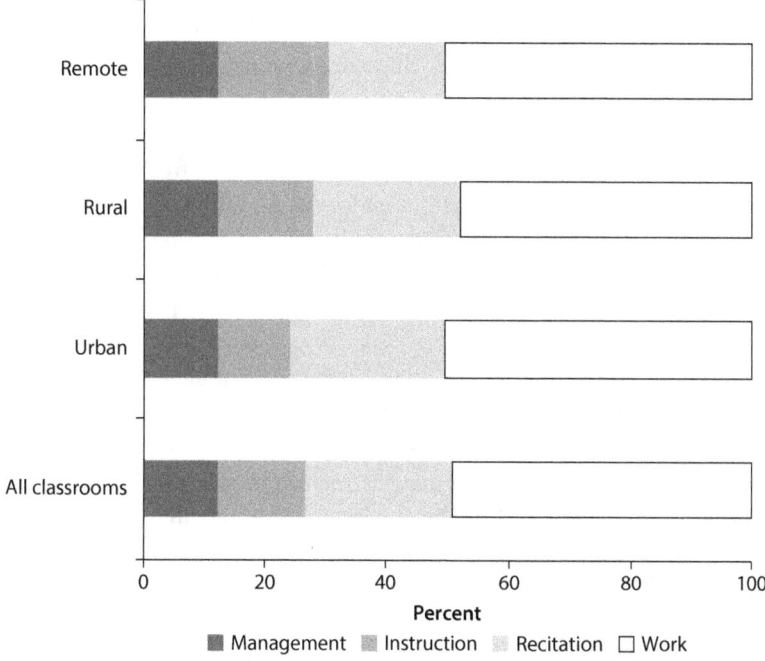

Source: World Bank 2012a.

Figure 4.12 Time Segments by Class Period (1–3)

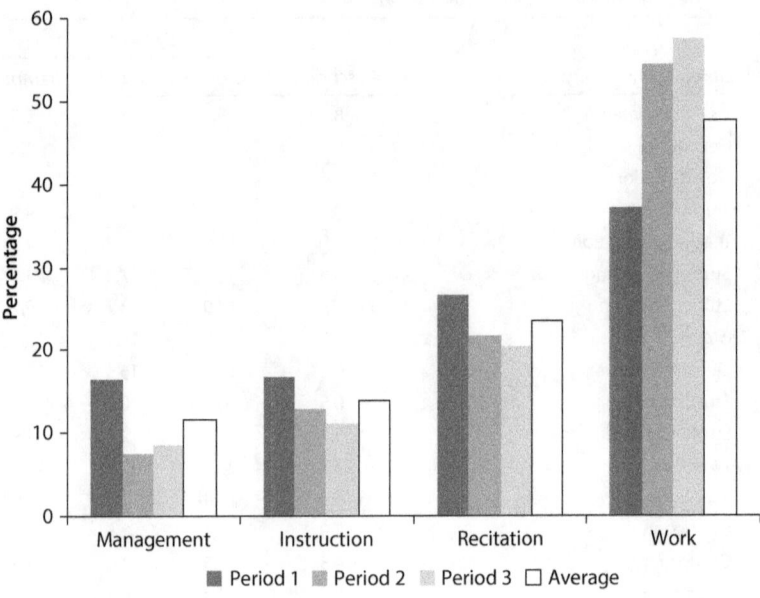

Source: World Bank 2012a.

spend much less time in instruction—more time is devoted to students working (figure 4.13).

Primary school classes, like TTC classes, thus exhibit a good mixture of activities, including instruction, work time, and recitation, and have coherent sequencing (figure 4.14).

How do Cambodian primary school classes compare with those in other countries? This study's data can be compared with data from the widely used Stallings instrument (box 4.2). There are four main Stallings time use categories: active instruction (for example, teacher explaining, answering/asking questions); passive instruction (students copying or reading); classroom management (for example, dealing with discipline); and teacher off-task (for example, teacher out of room).

The typical Cambodian class time use is near the Stallings good practice indicator standard for instruction, but off-track in classroom management and teacher off-task (figure 4.13). This standard is 50 percent active instruction, 35 percent passive instruction, 15 percent management, and 0 percent off-task. The Cambodian overall average is 53.9 percent for active instruction (above the Stallings good practice standard), 34.7 percent for passive instruction (identical to the standard), 6.5 percent for management (less than the standard), and 6 percent off-task (higher than the standard). These proportions vary little among urban, rural, and remote classrooms. But time segment summaries alone cannot suffice as quality indicators.

Figure 4.13 Time Segments Using Stallings Observation Categories

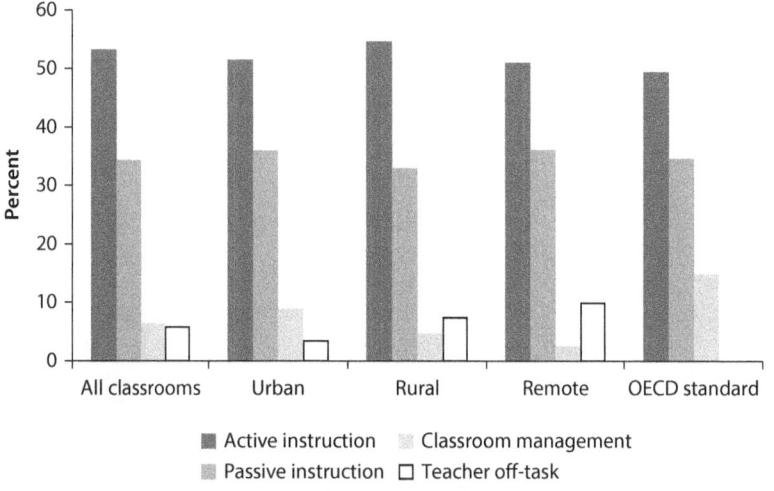

Source: World Bank 2012a.
Note: OECD = Organisation for Economic Co-operation and Development.

Box 4.2 What Is the Stallings Method?

The Stallings method uses a standardized coding grid to register the activities and materials teachers and students use during a single class. Ten 15-second observations or "snapshots" are made at regular intervals.

In these 15 seconds, the observer scans the room in a 360-degree circle starting with the teacher and codes four key aspects of classroom dynamics in detail: class time use—instruction, classroom management, or other activities (considered off-task); pedagogical practices; learning materials; and share of students visibly engaged in teacher-led activity and/or in off-task behaviors (such as social interaction with other students or tuned out). The Stallings method generates quantitative data and creates standardized measures of key variables. All Stallings results are expressed as a percentage of class time.

Source: World Bank 2011.

Teaching Activities

The post-lesson summaries provided by enumerators allow us to examine classroom activities in greater detail (table 4.24). As in TTC classes, teaching aids are not prevalent—they were used in only about 29 percent of the classrooms, and the figure is lower in remote areas. Encouragingly, students were observed using texts in almost every classroom.

Recitation is fairly prevalent but mostly involves teachers asking questions (table 4.25), usually of individual students rather than the whole class ("chorus" questions). In only 20 percent of the classes did teachers ask questions requiring

Figure 4.14 Comparison of Time Segments in Primary Schools, TTCs, and Baseline Survey

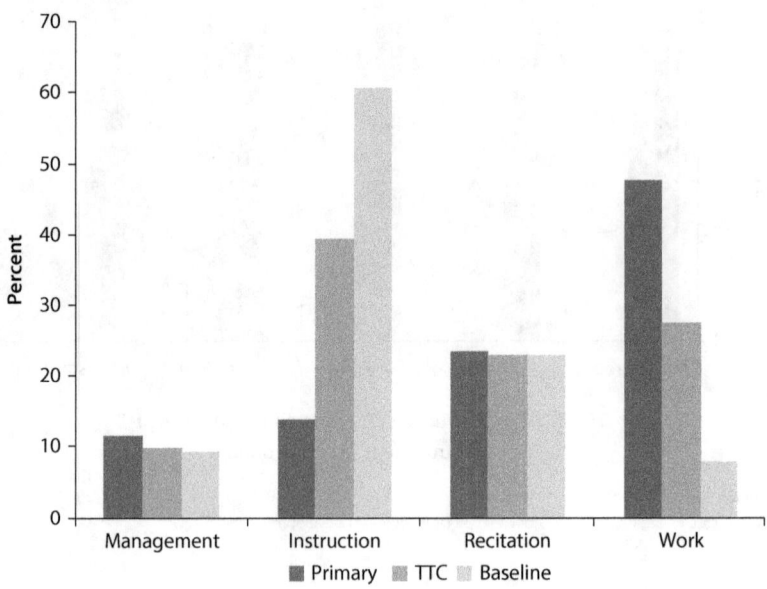

Sources: CESSP Baseline Survey 2006; World Bank 2012a, 2012b.
Note: TTC = teaching training center.

imagination or creativity and in only about 17 percent did students ask teachers questions. In about 40 percent (55 percent in remote schools), teachers did not ask students to give their opinions. These interactions suggest a fairly teacher-centered dynamic.

Other data also suggest a teacher-centered dynamic. Both students and teachers use blackboards often, for example, but in many schools only the teacher does so (table 4.26). Teachers also write lessons onto the blackboard for students to copy. This practice may be problematic, especially if it is not accompanied by explanation and work activities. In about 10 percent of classes, the teachers did not ask students to demonstrate their learning of the lesson. In remote schools, this proportion was 37.2 percent, suggesting that teachers in these locations are less active in verifying student learning.

Teacher Standards

As in TTCs, teacher standards have not been embedded into the primary school system. Only about half of teachers have heard of the teacher standards, and about 25 percent have had them explained. Much work remains in adapting the standards to the average primary school classroom, including teacher training, support, and evaluation activities around these standards (figure 4.15). Teachers who have heard of them (or have had them explained) are likely to indicate that the standards have "a significant" influence on their teaching, suggesting that teachers will respond positively to exposure to the standards.

Table 4.24 Teaching Materials (Classroom Observations)
Percent, unless otherwise indicated

Variable	All schools	By location		
		Urban	Rural	Remote
Teacher used teaching aids	29.0	38.8	22.4	18.6
Students used textbooks	86.5	84.7	87.7	88.6
Sample size (number)	284	55	202	26

Source: World Bank 2012a.
Note: All results are based on weighted data.

Table 4.25 Questions and Feedback (Classroom Observations)
Percent, unless otherwise indicated

Variable	All schools	By location		
		Urban	Rural	Remote
Teacher question types				
Collectively ("chorus")	44.9	58.6	34.6	45.3
Individually	92.3	93.6	92.0	83.1
That require imagination	21.0	21.3	21.3	13.3
Students ask questions?	16.7	8.1	23.7	7.6
Teacher feedback				
Praise or encouragement				
Never	24.3	20.3	28.0	16.5
Once	11.5	9.0	12.1	28.8
More than once	64.2	70.8	59.9	54.6
Correcting a mistake				
Never	22.6	16.2	27.2	26.5
Once	11.0	11.7	9.1	28.8
More than once	66.5	72.1	63.8	44.7
Scolding or critical				
Never	84.6	85.4	84.1	82.8
Once	9.4	9.5	9.5	6.8
More than once	6.0	5.1	6.4	10.4
Asked student to give opinion				
Never	42.6	40.0	43.7	55.4
Once	10.4	13.6	7.5	13.7
More than once	47.0	46.4	48.8	30.9
Sample size (number)	284	55	202	26

Source: World Bank 2012a.
Note: All results are based on weighted data.

Teacher Quality Factor Analysis

How are these measures of teacher capacity and methodology related? What do they indicate about teaching quality? We use factor analysis to see if the teachers who take attendance and have lesson plans, for example, also score the highest

Figure 4.15 Teachers and Teacher Standards

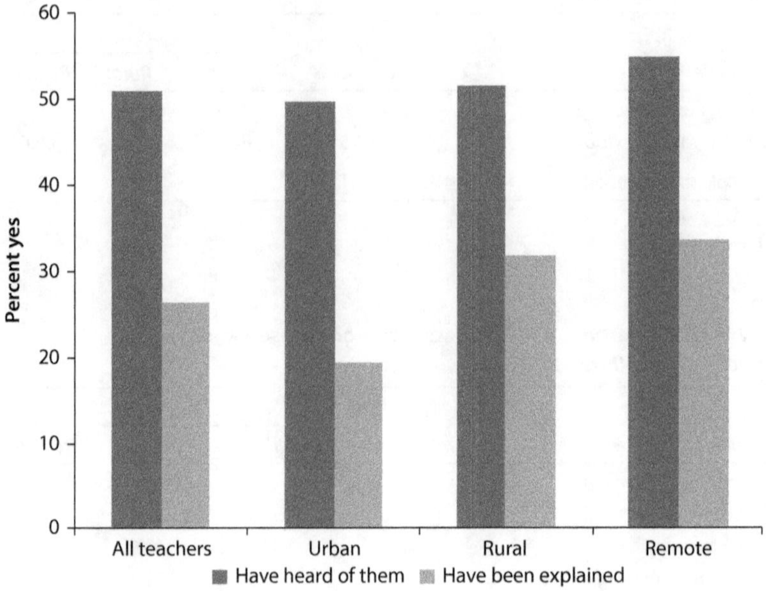

[Bar chart showing "Percent yes" for "Have heard of them" and "Have been explained" across All teachers, Urban, Rural, and Remote categories. All teachers: ~51%, ~27%. Urban: ~50%, ~20%. Rural: ~52%, ~32%. Remote: ~55%, ~34%.]

Source: World Bank 2012a.

Table 4.26 Work Activities (Classroom Observations)
Percent, unless otherwise indicated

		By location		
Variable	All schools	Urban	Rural	Remote
Blackboard used by				
Only teacher	31.6	26.6	35.2	32.4
Teacher and students	67.3	73.4	62.9	67.6
Teacher copied lesson from text onto board	81.1	76.0	84.6	87.9
Teacher summarized lesson/explanation/discussion on board	83.5	86.4	82.0	77.3
Teacher wrote questions on board to copy				
Never	16.7	16.6	16.7	18.9
Once	22.0	19.2	23.8	23.8
More than once	61.3	64.2	59.5	57.3
Teacher had students carry out task to demonstrate learning of lesson				
Never	9.6	4.9	11.0	37.2
Once	15.2	15.1	14.8	18.9
More than once	75.2	80.0	74.3	43.9
Teacher used students' names				
Never	4.4	4.2	4.9	0
Rarely	4.4	3.2	5.4	4.3
Usually	29.0	24.2	33.9	14.7
Always	62.1	68.4	55.8	81.0
Sample size (number)	284	55	202	26

Source: World Bank 2012a.
Note: All results are based on weighted data.

on mathematics tests (see chapter 5) or use more instruction in their classes. We analyze the correlations between variables to determine if the measures indicate latent traits.

Many classroom process variables show correlations with good practices in classroom behavior (table 4.27). The most positive loadings relate to asking students questions individually, monitoring the class throughout the lesson, giving praise frequently, students giving their opinions frequently, and using recitation and group work in the lesson. The teacher's content and PCK have positive loadings, but they are fairly modest compared with other indicators.

The active instruction Stallings category is correlated with higher student achievement (appendix figures D.1 and D.2), particularly in Khmer. To evaluate the classroom observation data, we incorporate two strategies. For the first factor, we use the Stallings categories from above (see figure 4.15); for the second, we use the individual time segment categories instead of the categorical summaries. The results show that passive instruction has a large negative loading factor, consistent with the individual (negative) loadings for copying and seatwork. The results also show that teachers who have received the good teaching performance award do not score significantly higher (or lower), raising questions about the award's utility.

Student Achievement Multivariate Analysis

Factor analysis did not show much correlation between teacher variables and student achievement; multivariate analysis can test this correlation more rigorously (appendix tables E.1–E.7). Although explicit causality cannot be established, and individual student scores cannot be matched to individual teachers, all teacher and classroom observation variables in the multivariate analysis represent school averages.

Consistent with previous statistical analysis of student achievement in Cambodia, many of these controls predict student achievement in grade 3 (appendix table E.1). This analysis includes gender (boys score higher than girls), socioeconomic status, student absences, and school fees (positive). The baseline model includes student, family, and community variables.

Teacher Questionnaire Variables

Further analysis suggests that three teaching variables correlate strongly with student achievement (appendix table E.2): teacher standards, quality teacher technical meetings, and a transparent teacher evaluation system. The first two, especially teacher standards, are correlated with raised achievement in Khmer, and the third is correlated with raised achievement in math. Teachers with second jobs outside of teaching are correlated with lower achievement in both subjects, especially in math. Follow-up studies linking students and teachers with learning outcomes can shed further light on these correlations.

There is no evidence that teacher incentives improve student achievement (appendix table E.2). In fact, schools with more remote placement bonuses have

Table 4.27 Factor Analysis of Teacher Quality

Variable	Factor loadings		Correlation with achievement	
	Factor 1	Factor 2	Khmer	Maths
Takes attendance	−0.04	−0.03	0.13	0.03
Has a lesson plan	0.14	0.17	0.17	0.10
Uses teacher aids	0.23	0.31	0.20	0.12
Asks creative questions	0.41	0.34	0.02	−0.01
Asks individual questions	0.46	0.46	0.04	−0.08
Students ask questions	0.25	0.23	−0.08	−0.07
Uses group work	0.16	0.35	0.13	0.05
Monitors the class	0.46	0.52	0.11	−0.03
Frequency gives praise	0.44	0.54	0.13	0.01
Frequency corrects	0.40	0.49	−0.09	−0.19
Frequency students give opinion	0.39	0.45	0.01	−0.08
Uses blackboard to demonstrate example	0.22	0.37	0.15	0.12
Heard of teacher standards	0.14	0.17	0.09	0.04
Content knowledge	0.21	0.23	0.03	−0.02
PCK	0.20	0.22	−0.07	−0.09
Teaching segments (%)				
Control of class	—	−0.06	0.21	0.24
No instruction	—	−0.20	−0.01	0.11
Instruction	—	0.17	−0.01	0.01
Copying	—	−0.55	−0.32	−0.17
Reading	—	0.12	0.02	−0.01
Recitation	—	0.39	0.08	−0.04
Seatwork	—	−0.06	0.16	0.10
Discussion	—	0.03	0.20	0.20
Group work	—	0.34	0.16	0.07
Stallings categories				
Active instruction	**0.76**	—	0.16	0.07
Passive instruction	−0.67	—	−0.13	−0.07
Management	−0.08	—	0.23	0.25
Off-task	−0.25	—	−0.24	−0.16
Factor 1	—	—	0.17	−0.01
Factor 2	—	—	0.15	−0.01
Eigenvalue	2.53	2.51	—	—
Explained variance	0.34	0.26	—	—
Sample size (number)	268	268	149	149

Source: World Bank 2012a.
Note: PCK = pedagogical content knowledge. Boldface used to highlight significant differences. — = or eigenvalue/explained. Variance statistic is not applicable (correlation summary).

significantly lower achievement in Khmer, even when controlling for location and poverty. The impact of the deployment bonus was analyzed in more detail with a statistical interaction term between teacher deployment bonus and the teacher's home province. Student achievement improves when teachers from different provinces receive the placement bonus, but the variable is not significant.

Classroom Observations

Some covariates correlate positively with student learning. Schools where textbooks are used more frequently have higher Khmer language achievement in grade three (appendix table E.5). Passive instruction and off-topic time lower achievement, especially in Khmer language, underscoring the need for more efficient class time use.

Teaching and Learning Environment: Student Interview

As expected, more opportunities to participate in class and go to the blackboard raise student achievement (appendix table E.6). Student achievement decreases when the teacher is often angry. However, some of these results could be driven by differences among students within each school rather than differences among schools.

Notes

1. Interview, MoEYS, July 2013.
2. MoEYS defines 120 districts in 23 provinces as disadvantaged areas and seven provinces as remote provinces (Ratana Kiri, Mondol Kiri, Stung Treng, Odor Meanchey, Preah Vihear, Koh Kong, and Pailin).

Bibliography

Benveniste, Luis, Jeffery Marshall, and M. Caridad Aranjo. 2008. *Teaching in Cambodia*. Washington, DC: World Bank.

Brehm, William, Iveta Silova, and Tuot Mono. 2012. "Hidden Privatization of Public Education in Cambodia: The Impact and Implications of Private Tutoring." ESP Working Paper Series 39, Open Society Foundation, Washington, DC.

Cambodia Administrative Reform General Secretariat. 2010. *Yearbook*.

CESSP (Cambodia Education Sector Support Project).

Marcelo, Carlos. 2002. "Learning to Teach in the Knowledge Society: Literature Review." Working paper, World Bank, Washington, DC.

Rowan, Brian, Stephen G. Schilling, Deborah L. Ball, and Robert Miller. 2001. *Measuring Teachers' Pedagogical Content Knowledge in Surveys: An Exploratory Study*. Philadelphia, PA: Consortium for Policy Research in Education.

Shulman, Lee S. 1986. "Those Who Understand: Knowledge Growth in Teaching." *Educational Researcher* 15 (2): 4–14.

World Bank. 2006. *Cambodia Education Sector Support Project Baseline Survey*. Washington, DC: World Bank.

———. 2011. *Conducting Classroom Observations: Manual and User Guide for Measuring Instructional Time in Class*. Washington, DC.

———. 2012a. "Teacher Survey." World Bank, Washington, DC.

———. 2012b. "School Director Survey." World Bank, Washington, DC.

CHAPTER 5

Teacher Outcomes: Mathematics and Pedagogical Content Knowledge in the Teaching Force

Key Messages

Teacher training center (TTC) trainers, trainees, and teachers in service have alarmingly low mathematics knowledge. Their mathematics scores—at about or slightly above that of an average grade 9 student—raise serious concerns. Trainees also know more mathematics than their trainers in all subject areas.

Regional teacher training center (RTTC) trainees and TTC trainers who are mathematics specialists are more knowledgeable. But even this group shows weaknesses—TTC trainer mathematics knowledge averages only about 75 percent.

Years of education correlate strongly with mathematics knowledge. Provincial teacher training center (PTTC) trainees in the 12+2 tranche score significantly higher than their 9+2 counterparts, for example, suggesting the need to require 12 years of education before PTTC entry.

Trainers, trainees, and teachers in service also lack proficiency in pedagogical content knowledge (PCK). Many struggle to diagnose basic student errors, an important aspect of effective teaching. And the specialists do not score much higher in PCK than their nonspecialist counterparts. TTCs must provide greater PCK as well as content knowledge.

Trainer and Trainee Mathematics Knowledge

Research on what constitutes effective teacher education programs has focused on two key areas: subject knowledge and PCK. The first stresses subject-specific knowledge possessed by teachers, such as math or language, as a key driver of teacher effectiveness and student achievement (Marcelo 2002). When pooled with knowledge about individual students, classroom management, school learning environment, and pedagogy and evaluation, this knowledge correlates strongly with student learning outcomes. PCK, specialized knowledge about teaching and learning in a particular discipline, also correlates strongly with student achievement.[1] Improving PCK can greatly improve teachers' professional development and effectiveness (Darling-Hammond 2002; Marcelo 2002).

We measured trainer and trainee mathematics knowledge directly, using a 30-question instrument divided into the following components:

- Six mathematics content knowledge questions drawn from previous national grade 6 assessments
- Twelve mathematics content knowledge questions drawn from previous national grade 9 assessments
- Six mathematics content knowledge questions drawn from the Trends in International Mathematics and Science Study (TIMSS) 2008 public grade 8 items
- Six PCK questions on applied mathematics knowledge, combining content and pedagogical components

These assessments enabled us to address several important questions, such as the following:

- Do teacher trainees and teachers in service know more mathematics than grades 6 and 9 students?
- How do RTTC and PTTC trainees compare in knowledge?
- Do TTC trainers know more mathematics than TTC trainees?
- How do these comparisons vary depending on specialization and mathematics area, especially for RTTC trainees, who are subject specialists, and trainers?
- What factors correlate with more or less mathematics knowledge?

Overall, mathematics knowledge is alarmingly low. On average, trainers score roughly the same as an average grade 9 Cambodian student on mathematics knowledge; trainees score slightly higher. A significant portion of trainers, trainees, and teachers in service lack the skills to diagnose the mistakes students make and propose adequate solutions, raising concerns about classroom effectiveness.

Mathematics Knowledge Comparisons

Three themes emerge.

First, low grade 9 mathematics scores show that mathematics knowledge is inadequate (table 5.1 and figure 5.1; for more detail, see appendix table E.7). Teacher trainees should know grade 9 mathematics, regardless of their specialization (for RTTC trainees), even if they end up teaching early grades in primary schools. These results are consistent with those from national assessments (CESSP Baseline Survey various years), and highlight the importance of improving basic education.

These concerns are partially validated by the mathematics results from the 2008 TIMSS (table 5.1). The overall percentages correct (between 54 and

Table 5.1 Teacher Trainer and Trainee Mathematics and Pedagogical Content Knowledge

	Full sample comparisons			PTTC trainee subsamples			Trainer subsamples	
Mathematics result	RTTC trainees	PTTC trainees	Trainers	12+2	9+2	Remote	RTTC	PTTC
Content items	67.9*	60.4	53.4*	67.0	50.2*	53.5	53.0	53.6
	(19.5)	(18.4)	(20.8)	(17.0)	(15.5)	(17.1)	(24.8)	(19.1)
Pedagogical content knowledge	70.3*	70.8	57.9*	72.1	68.8	69.8	61.0	55.9
	(14.8)	(12.7)	(22.9)	(12.9)	(12.0)	(12.2)	(18.0)	(24.6)
TIMSS	64.2	61.8	54.4*	66.7	54.1*	59.4	55.4	53.8
	(24.8)	(22.8)	(29.2)	(20.6)	(24.1)	(24.5)	(36.2)	(26.0)
Overall score	68.4*	65.5	55.7*	69.4	59.6*	62.1	57.1	54.7
	(14.3)	(12.9)	(19.1)	(12.5)	(11.1)	(12.2)	(20.6)	(18.5)
IRT equated score G9	592.8*	562.5	501.8*	592.2	516.7*	534.0	518.4	491.1
	(127.3)	(98.2)	(133.9)	(102.4)	(70.6)	(79.8)	(153.9)	(124.9)
IRT equated score G9 (content only)	602.6*	558.7	525.5	591.4	508.2*	525.3	532.7	521.0
	(133.8)	(95.0)	(134.1)	(93.2)	(73.5)	(80.6)	(187.0)	(107.1)
IRT equated score G6	807.1*	759.4	663.7	806.1	687.1*	714.4	689.8	646.8
	(200.7)	(154.8)	(211.0)	(161.3)	(111.3)	(125.8)	(242.5)	(196.9)
Sample size	301	651	102	387	264	257	30	72

Source: World Bank 2012a.
Note: IRT = item response theory; PTTC = provincial teacher training center; RTTC = regional teacher training center; TIMSS = Trends in International Mathematics and Science Study. Numbers in parentheses indicate standard deviation. * = significant at .05 level.

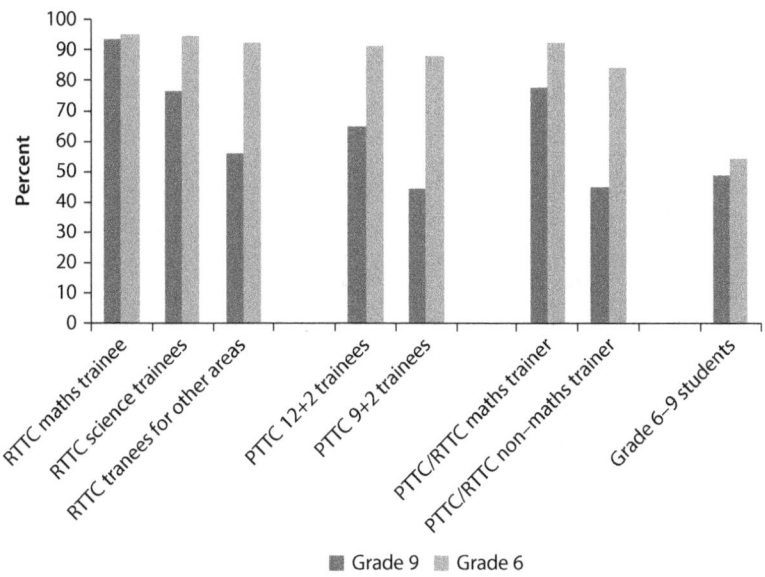

Figure 5.1 Knowledge of Grades 6 and 9 Common Math Items

Source: World Bank 2012a.
Note: PTTC = provincial teacher training center; RTTC = regional teacher training center.

64 percent) again suggest low average achievement. The TIMSS items, intended for grade 8 students, were not among the more difficult questions.

Second, teacher trainees exhibit more mathematics knowledge than their trainers in all three categories (mathematics, PCK, and TIMSS items) (figure 5.2). RTTC trainees have the most mathematics knowledge, followed by PTTC trainees and then the trainers. How large is the trainee advantage? For the grades 6 and 9 content items, the RTTC trainees score about 0.75 of one standard deviation higher than the trainers, while PTTC trainees are about one-third of a standard deviation higher. For the PCK and TIMSS items, the differences are not as large, but still significant. This translates into an overall difference ("overall score") of nearly one standard deviation between RTTC trainees and trainers and about 0.75 standard deviation between PTTC trainees and the average trainer. More recent exposure to the curriculum is probably not the sole reason, especially since trainees also scored higher than trainers on the PCK questions.

Although they score higher than their trainers, trainees do not score much higher than an average grade 9 student. But TTC trainees and trainers score significantly higher than the average grade 6 student on grade 6 mathematics. Not surprisingly, math specialists have the highest results. For grade 9 mathematics, the differences between trainers, trainees, and grade 9 students are not as pronounced. RTTC trainees answered about 64 percent of the grade 9 math items correctly, suggesting that the average RTTC trainee is not entirely comfortable

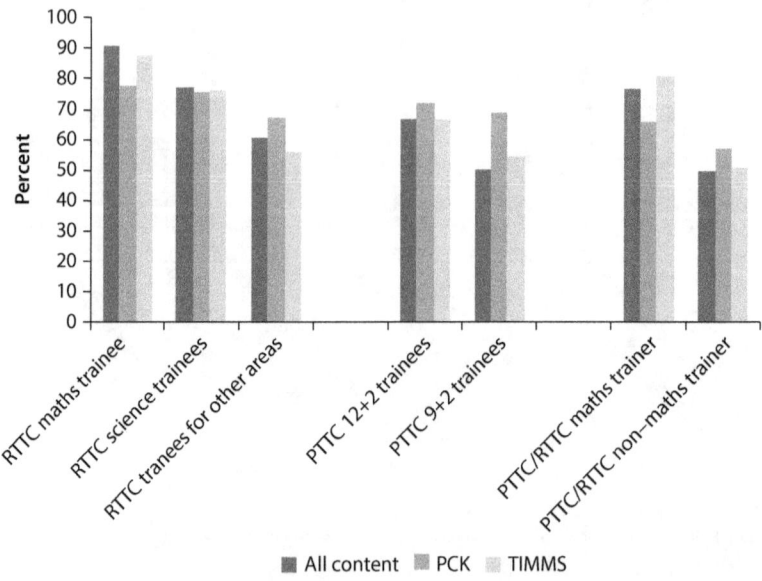

Figure 5.2 Content, PCK, and TIMSS Averages

Source: World Bank 2012a.
Note: PCK = pedagogical content knowledge; PTTC = provincial teacher training center; RTTC = regional teacher training center; TIMSS = Trends in International Mathematics and Science Study.

with this content. The PTTC trainees scored lower (about 58 percent), and the TTC trainers scored about the same as the grade 9 students.

Third, there are significant performance disparities among trainees: PTTC trainees in the 12+2 program have more mathematics knowledge than their 9+2 counterparts. The 12+2 advantage applies only to the content items (grades 6 and 9 and TIMSS), not the PCK questions, and probably results from added exposure to mathematics in grades 10–12.

Encouragingly, remote and nonremote PTTC trainees do not differ widely in mathematics knowledge. Nor do RTTC and PTTC trainers, suggesting similar background and training levels. But a key question is whether or not math and science specialists score higher on these items.

Across the three tested domains (grade 6/9 content, PCK, and TIMSS), RTTC mathematics trainees and, to a lesser extent, RTTC science trainees, have the highest scores. They are followed by trainers who are mathematics specialists. The lowest scores are for RTTC nonmath and nonscience trainees, PTTC 9+2 trainees, and nonmath trainers.

Examining Teaching Knowledge

Content knowledge alone is insufficient for effective teaching. Teachers must also develop specialized knowledge about the mistakes students make and effective solutions.

The questions presented in box 5.1 cover a straightforward problem faced by a math teacher. The student, George, is not correctly applying the regrouping (or borrowing) property to his mathematics problems. He is doing it automatically, regardless of whether or not the number in the single units column is larger than the number in the tens column. As a result, in some cases he gets the wrong answer, but his answer is predictable because he is applying the rule in the same way in all problems.

In the first part of the activity, the TTC trainees and trainers were asked to identify which of the three problems George answered correctly (only the third problem). These first three questions reflect content knowledge and depend on whether or not the trainer or trainee understands the correct properties of subtraction. Most of the trainees and trainers could identify the incorrect and correct answers. For RTTC and PTTC trainees, the averages are in the 85–95 percent range, suggesting widespread knowledge of this basic subtraction. But the percentages for the TTC trainers are lower and show that only about 80 percent of them were able to correctly identify George's correct and incorrect answers.

The two questions in the bottom of box 5.1 reflect more explicitly PCK. These questions require the trainee/trainer to both understand the mistake George is committing in the three problems he answered and apply this mistake to these two new problems to assess whether his approach will result in the correct or incorrect response. (The answer is that George's incorrect application of the carrying property will not matter in the first problem, and he will obtain the correct answer. But in the second problem he will probably not arrive at the correct answer.)

Box 5.1 PCK Item 7

George recently learned to regroup (or "to borrow"), and at first he got correct answers. But soon there were difficulties. Take a look at his test paper and tables B5.1.1 and B5.1.2.

Name: George

A. 187 − 43 = 1414   B. 186 − 23 = 1413   C. 384 − 59 = 325

Which exercise is (are) correct and which exercise is (are) incorrect?
(Circle 1 or 2 to indicate CORRECT or INCORRECT for each exercise.)

Table B5.1.1 Percentage Correct for Each PCK Item (7A–7C)

PCK Item	Full samples			PTTC subsamples			Trainer subsamples	
	RTTC	PTTC	Trainers	12+2	9+2	Remote	RTTC	PTTC
7A. Exercise A (Incorrect)	94.6	96.1*	78.7*	96.6	95.3	95.5	86.7	73.6
7B. Exercise B (Incorrect)	94.6*	94.1	81.7*	94.8	93.2	92.1	90.0	76.4*
7C. Exercise C (Correct)	86.3	85.0	77.8*	85.0	85.1	84.9	80.0	76.4

Note: PCK = pedagogical content knowledge; PTTC = provincial teacher training center; RTTC = regional teacher training center.

Which of the following problems is George likely to get correct using his procedure? (Look again at his working above to answer this question.)

Circle 1 or 2 to indicate CORRECT or INCORRECT for each problem.

Table B5.1.2 Percentage Correct for Each PCK Item (7D–7E)

PCK Item	Full samples			PTTC subsamples			Trainer subsamples	
	RTTC	PTTC	Trainers	12+2	9+2	Remote	RTTC	PTTC
7D. 273 − 38 (Correct)	59.9	65.5	57.3	67.1	62.9	66.5	60.0	55.6
7E. 285 − 63 (Incorrect)	54.5	54.7	48.3	58.3	49.1	51.6	50.0	47.2

Note: PCK = pedagogical content knowledge; PTTC = provincial teacher training center; RTTC = regional teacher training center.
* = significant at 0.5.

When the question requires more explicitly PCK, the percentage of trainees and trainers who obtain the correct answers is substantially lower. On average only about 60 percent of the respondents answered each question correctly, and there are no significant differences between trainees and trainers.

What do these results say about mathematics teaching capacity among TTC trainees and trainers? First, trainees and, to a lesser degree, trainers are fairly comfortable with basic mathematics. But some trainees—and even more of the trainers—are stumbling on basic content questions.

In primary level mathematics, trainees and trainers lack specialized teaching knowledge, or the ability to diagnose the student problems they encounter (Hill, Ball, and Schilling 2008). This finding raises concerns about teaching quality. The low results for trainers raise questions about TTC ability to train teachers, regardless of how much emphasis is given to these aspects of teaching. Many trainees will have to acquire this PCK in practice as they encounter problems in their day-to-day work and look for solutions.

Subject-Specialist Comparisons

There are reasons to be concerned about mathematics knowledge among trainees and trainers throughout the teacher training system. For the RTTC trainees, and the trainers in PTTCs and RTTCs, this issue should be explored based on specialization. Mathematics knowledge is not as important for an RTTC trainee who expects to teach English or Khmer.

RTTC trainees who are mathematics specialists score the highest on all three measures—content knowledge, PCK, and overall average (figure 5.3). How large is the math specialist advantage? The mathematics trainee overall average of 84 percent is about 1.8 standard deviations higher than RTTC trainees who are specialists in Khmer, English, or social sciences—a very large difference.

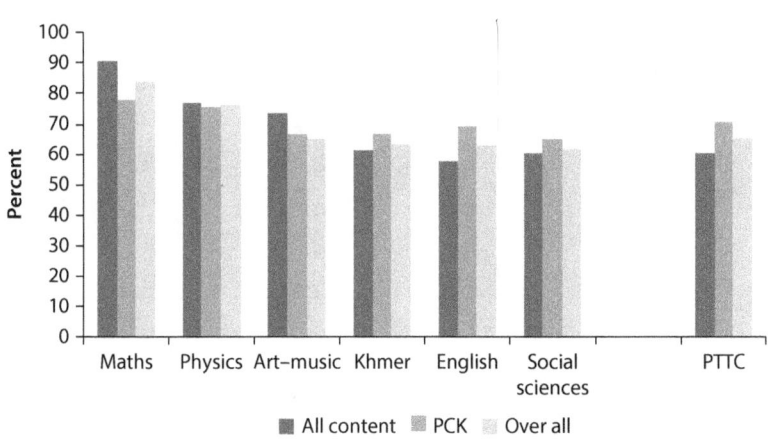

Figure 5.3 RTTC Trainee Mathematics Knowledge by Teaching Specialization

Source: World Bank 2012a.
Note: PCK = pedagogical content knowledge; PTTC = provincial teacher training center; RTTC = regional teacher training center.

This is encouraging, as it shows that future mathematics teachers have the most mathematics knowledge.

PCK averages are fairly compressed across subject specializations (figure 5.3). The highest scoring category (mathematics specialists) is only about 14 percent higher than the lowest categories, a much smaller spread than in the content knowledge questions. The compression may be explained by the fact that the PCK questions do not depend solely on mathematics knowledge. Nonspecialists can answer these questions by applying other skills.

Trainer mathematics knowledge by training specialization is very similar to that of RTTC trainees (figure 5.4). But trainers' overall mathematics knowledge is lower. TTC trainers who are mathematics specialists have the most math knowledge in all three reported measures, although their 76 percent average score on the content items appears low. Math trainer specialists' overall knowledge average is about 1.5 standard deviations higher than the lowest trainer category scores. This difference is especially pronounced in the content items, where the spread between math specialists and art/music trainers is just over 40 percentage points.

PCK averages are much more even across categories. Math specialists have the most PCK (about 65 percent), but their advantage over art/music teachers is only about 15 percent. Psychology-pedagogy specialists have the second highest average on PCK items. Their scores are the same as those of the math specialists, although their mathematics knowledge is substantially lower (76.7 versus 50.1 percent). This finding provides some indirect validation of the pedagogical content of the PCK questions, and demonstrates further that applied teaching knowledge does not depend entirely on content knowledge.

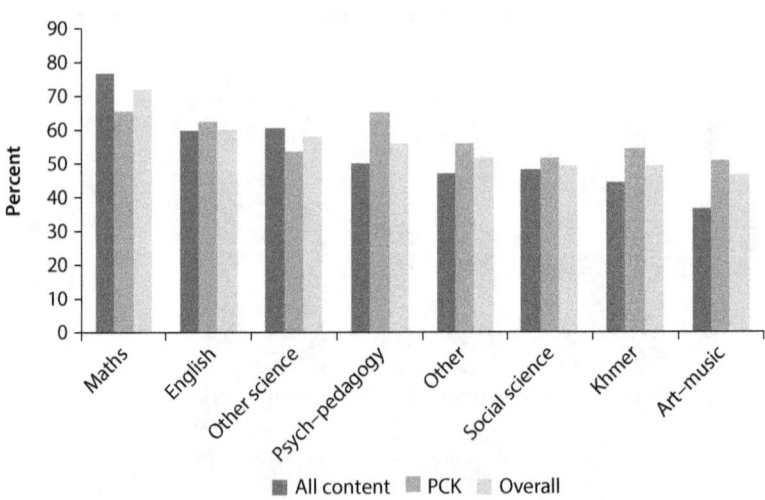

Figure 5.4 TTC Trainer Mathematics Knowledge by Training Specialization

Source: World Bank 2012a.
Note: PCK = pedagogical content knowledge; TTC = teacher training center.

Comparing Assessments

Exit examinations provide additional evidence. Indeed, it is important to know if students who performed best on the mathematics questions in the external data collection also score the highest on the exit examinations. This matters because very few students fail the exit examination. But these scores influence which schools graduates can select, as the highest scoring students can choose urban schools or the schools with the best reputations.

By reviewing the exit examination results for PTTC and RTTC trainees, taken shortly after the external data collection, we can assess consistency across assessment sources. But there are caveats. First, the data for this study focus only on mathematics. Second, exit examination results suffer the same limitations as teacher-assigned notes or grades: in theory they reflect absolute standards, but in reality they are based more on relative performance. So scores are not comparable across training centers.

For PTTC trainees, who will be responsible for all subjects in their primary schools, the exit examination results include pedagogy, Khmer language, mathematics, science, and a total score (table 5.2). For RTTC trainees, there are only three scores available: pedagogy, a total score, and a subject specialty score. The RTTC subject score (not presented) corresponds to the RTTC trainee's specialization area (figure 5.5).[2]

Exit examination results show little variation across trainee category. Most scores average about 7 (the highest scores are 9.5). PTTC trainees in the 12+2 tranche score significantly higher in mathematics and science and in their total scores than the 9+2 trainees. PTTC trainees in remote TTCs score significantly

Table 5.2 Exit Examination Results

Variable	Full samples		PTTC subsamples		
	RTTC	PTTC	12+2	9+2	Remote
Exit exam scores					
Pedagogy	6.9	6.7	7.0	6.2	**6.0***
	(0.9)	(1.1)	(1.1)	(1.0)	(1.0)
Khmer	—	7.2	7.2	7.4	7.2
		(1.0)	(1.0)	(1.0)	(1.1)
Mathematics	—	7.1	7.6	**6.4***	6.4
		(1.3)	(1.1)	(1.2)	(1.4)
Science	—	7.3	7.6	**6.8***	7.1
		(0.9)	(0.9)	(0.7)	(0.9)
Total score	28.9	43.0	44.4	**41.0***	41.0
	(2.3)	(3.8)	(3.4)	(3.2)	(3.7)
Sample size (number)	298	649	386	263	255

Source: World Bank 2012a.

Note: All results are based on weighted data. Standard deviations are in parentheses. Tests of significance are used to compare 12+2 and 9+2 averages (significant differences highlighted in 9+2 column), and remote and nonremote PTTC averages (highlighted in remote column). PTTC = provincial teacher training center; RTTC = regional teacher training center; — = scores are not available for RTTC trainees.

* = Difference in average/percentage is significantly different at 0.05 level (two-tail); + = Difference in average/percentage is significantly different at 0.10 level. Boldface also used to highlight significant differences.

Figure 5.5 RTTC Exit Examination Results by Specialization Area

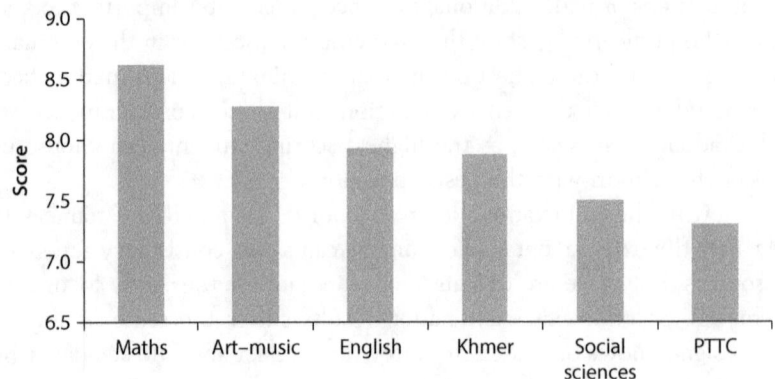

Source: Ministry of Education, Youth, and Sports 2012.
Note: PTTC = provincial teacher training center; RTTC = regional teacher training center;

lower in pedagogy, the only major difference from their nonremote counterparts. Math specialists scored the highest subject-specialty averages, followed by art/music trainees. Physics specialists scored the lowest.

There is a moderate but significant correlation between the exit examination results and the TTC survey tests, although the correlation is weaker at the RTTC level (table 5.3). For example, the correlation between the total score on the exit examination and the overall average on the mathematics test is 0.34 for PTTC trainees and 0.14 for RTTC trainees. The correlation between PTTC mathematics exit examination scores and mathematics external test score is 0.37. Scores thus seem comparable across tests.

PCK results correlate more with content knowledge than with pedagogical knowledge on the exit examination. This is not surprising, given the specificity of the PCK items and their overlap with mathematics knowledge.

Multivariate Analysis

What individual and TTC characteristics correlate with mathematics and PCK? Why do some trainees and trainers score higher than others? The most likely explanations are education levels, specialization areas, and previous teaching experience.

According to multivariate analysis, the strongest correlational variables are gender, age, years of education, and subject specialty (table 5.4). Male trainees and trainers score consistently higher than their female counterparts, even when controlling for years of education. The male advantage is larger for RTTC trainees and trainers. Age significantly lowers mathematics knowledge, particularly among PTTC trainees. One of the most significant predictors of mathematics knowledge is years of education, measured in two ways: one for total years of education, and another for PTTC students in the 12+2 tranche. The first measure is consistently positive and significant. The coefficients suggest that each year of

Table 5.3 Correlation Matrix for Exit Examination and Mathematics Test Results

	Exit examination components					Math test		
Variable	Pedag.	Khmer	Maths	Science	Total	Content	PCK	Total
PTTC trainees								
Pedagogy	—							
Khmer	−0.02	—						
Math	**0.37***	**0.12***	—					
Science	**0.42***	0.07	**0.29***	—				
Total	**0.69***	**0.38***	**0.66***	**0.67***	—			
Content	**0.27***	−0.06	**0.40***	**0.26***	**0.37***	—		
PCK	**0.11***	−0.02	**0.20***	**0.12***	**0.18***	**0.45***	—	
Test total	**0.22***	−0.03	**0.37***	**0.25***	**0.34***	**0.87***	**0.77***	—
RTTC trainees								
Pedagogy	—							
Total	**0.66***	—	—	—	—			
Content	**0.11***	—	—	—	**0.14***	—		
PCK	0.04	—	—	—	0.06	**0.35***	—	
Test total	**0.11***	—	—	—	**0.14***	**0.84***	**0.76***	—
Math subject	0.26	—	—	—	**0.50***	0.04	−0.16	−0.06

Source: World Bank 2012a.
Note: Exit examination components refer to test results from TTC-applied exit exams (July 2012); Math test refers to results from tests applied as part of World Bank data collection in June 2012. Variables in vertical axis include exit examination components, followed by math test components. All coefficients represent Pearson's correlation coefficients; PCK = pedagogical content knowledge; PTTC = provincial teacher training center; RTTC = regional teacher training center; — = not available.
* = Difference in average/percentage is significantly different at 0.05 level (two-tail); Boldface also used to highlight significant differences.

education adds between 0.08 and 0.10 standard deviations to mathematics knowledge. But for the 12+2 versus 9+2 comparisons (for PTTC trainees) the impact is much larger: trainees in the 12+2 tranche score between 0.46 and 0.60 standard deviations higher than the 9+2 students. Since remote trainees are much more concentrated in the 9+2 category, this result raises concerns about the quality of teachers returning to their remote provinces to work.

These results reinforce the importance of providing trainees and trainers with adequate content knowledge. The 12+2 group results especially support requiring 12 years of education before entering PTTCs.

We also adapted the multivariate analysis to analyze PCK. The results are consistent with those for mathematics knowledge (appendix table E.7). Males and younger trainees score higher on PCK. Years of education are significant in some of the estimations. But the strongest predictors relate to specialty and previous math teaching experience.

Teacher Mathematics Knowledge

Applying the same instrument given to TTC trainers and trainees, we assessed teacher mathematics knowledge. The assessment included grades 6 and 9 mathematics knowledge, TIMSS items, and PCK questions.

Table 5.4 Mathematics Knowledge Covariates

Independent variable	Trainees-trainers (1)	(2)	PTTC trainees (3)	(4)	RTTC trainees (5)	(6)	Trainers (7)	(8)
Male	0.29** (3.53)	0.23** (3.72)	0.14 (1.66)	0.16+ (1.92)	0.45* (2.49)	0.23* (2.34)	0.43* (2.21)	0.43* (2.21)
Age	−0.08* (−2.42)	−0.07* (−2.77)	−0.07** (−6.07)	−0.07** (−4.55)	−0.11 (−1.81)	−0.08 (−1.57)	−0.02 (−0.60)	−0.02 (−0.60)
Years of education	0.08* (2.29)	0.08* (2.84)	0.09* (2.02)	0.07 (1.54)	0.02 (0.63)	0.04 (0.85)	0.10* (2.35)	0.10* (2.32)
Category: (excluded: PTTC 9+2)								
PTTC 12+2	0.60** (3.54)	0.58** (3.55)	0.57** (4.07)	0.46* (2.96)	—	—	—	—
RTTC	0.49** (3.37)	0.28+ (2.13)	—	—	—	—	−0.14 (−0.73)	−0.14 (−0.76)
Trainer	−0.27 (−0.80)	−0.34 (−1.38)	—	—	—	—	—	—
Experience teaching	0.06+ (2.02)	0.04 (1.69)	−0.15 (−1.12)	−0.14 (−1.30)	0.24** (4.84)	0.19* (2.41)	−0.01 (−0.31)	−0.01 (−0.30)
Worked as math teacher	—	—	—	—	—	—	1.69** (10.45)	1.68** (4.64)
Has copy of teacher standards	−0.13+ (−2.31)	−0.11 (−1.67)	−0.11 (−1.18)	−0.09 (−0.85)	0.32** (3.91)	0.35** (9.39)	−0.36 (−0.96)	−0.36 (−0.97)
Remote location	−0.06 (−0.67)	−0.09 (−0.89)	−0.16 (−1.60)	−0.05 (−0.49)	—	—	—	—
Math specialist	—	1.30** (12.76)	—	—	—	1.19** (11.12)	—	0.01 (0.02)
Exit exam results								
Math	—	—	—	0.13* (2.96)	—	—	—	—
Pedagogy	—	—	—	0.01 (0.05)	—	—	—	—
Total	—	—	—	—	0.07+ (2.05)	—	—	—
Sample size	1,050	1,050	649	649	299	299	102	102
Explained var. (R^2)	0.17	0.27	0.19	0.22	0.10	0.26	0.33	0.33

Source: World Bank 2012a.
Note: All results based on weighted data. Dependent variable is the standardized (z-score) overall average on externally-applied mathematics test. Coefficients represent change in standard deviations for each unit change in independent variable. For PTTC trainee estimations, parental education and grade 9 exam result were also included in models; these variables were insignificant. PTTC = provincial teacher training center; RTTC = regional teacher training center; — = Variable is not included in this estimation. of the statistical analysis due to categories not being appropriate, or data is not available.
Significance level: * = 0.05, ** = 0.01, + = 0.10.

Primary school teachers do not have substantial mathematics knowledge. They answered about half of the grades 6 and 9 items correctly (table 5.5). The PCK average is also near 50 percent, meaning that teachers could not resolve many teaching-related mathematics activities.

The average primary school teacher has a slightly lower equated score than the average grade 9 student (who averaged 500 points). Primary teachers scored much higher than the average grade 6 student—by nearly three standard deviations. The results raise concerns about mathematics knowledge, especially considering that teachers need to draw on multiple sources of content and teaching knowledge to prepare students.

The averages are not significantly different across school locations. Encouragingly, rural and remote primary teachers do not have less capacity than urban teachers, even though urban jobs are likely to be given to teachers with the highest exit examination scores or the most education. Scores are still low, however, for each teacher category.

Grades 5–6 teachers have substantially more knowledge than their grades 1–2 and 3–4 counterparts (figure 5.6). This finding suggests that more capable teachers

Table 5.5 Teacher Mathematics Knowledge

Variable	All schools	By location		
		Urban	Rural	Remote
Content items	51.8	55.0	49.0	53.3
	(21.8)	(20.4)	(22.0)	(23.2)
Pedagogical content knowledge	55.2	52.5	57.1	62.2
	(20.7)	(21.1)	(20.2)	(22.3)
TIMSS	47.7	48.1	46.8	54.4
	(29.0)	(29.4)	(28.7)	(28.0)
IRT equated score G9	484.9	482.6	484.7	516.0
	(96.4)	(90.5)	(93.9)	(122.4)
IRT equated score G6	777.2	779.1	776.7	763.3
	(109.0)	(98.9)	(110.4)	(112.5)

Source: World Bank 2012b.
Note: IRT = item response theory; TIMSS = Trends in International Mathematics and Science Study. All results are based on weighted data.

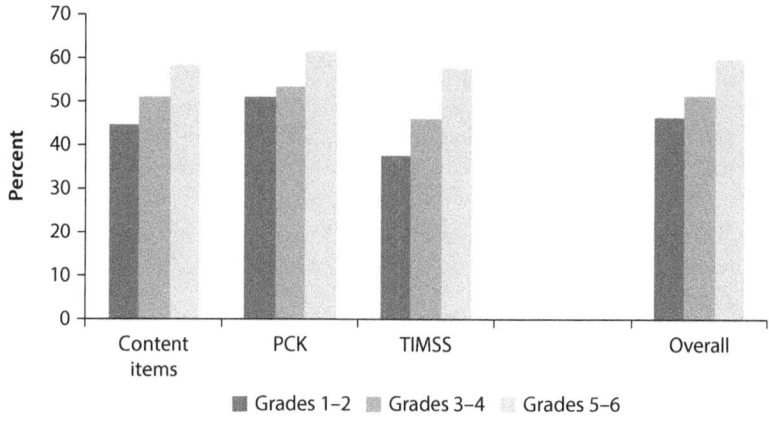

Figure 5.6 Teacher Mathematics Knowledge by Grade Level

Source: World Bank 2012b.
Note: PCK = pedagogical content knowledge; TIMSS = Trends in International Mathematics and Science Study.

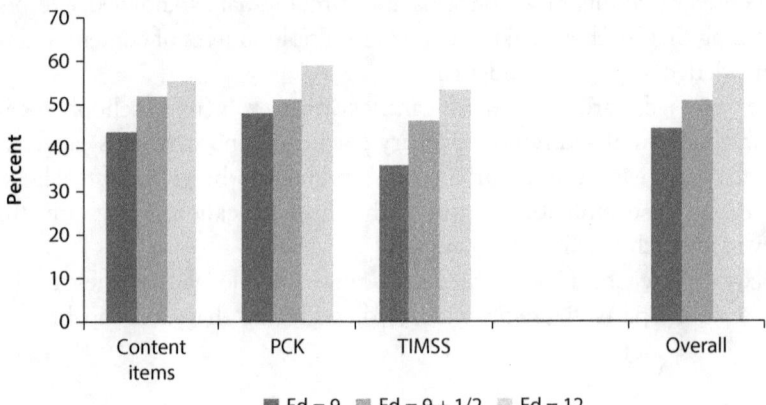

Figure 5.7 Teacher Mathematics Knowledge by Education Level

Source: World Bank 2012b.
Note: Ed = years of education; PCK = pedagogical content knowledge; TIMSS = Trends in International Mathematics and Science Study.

are being placed in higher grades or that their exposure to more mathematics in their daily teaching activities helps them with content and teaching knowledge.

Teachers may be learning on the job, but preservice education levels still matter: teachers with more years of schooling score higher on the assessment (figure 5.7). Years of formal education correlate with mathematics knowledge in all measures.

Notes

1. See Shulman (1986). As Rowan and others (2001) write, "pedagogical content knowledge is a form of practical knowledge that is used by teachers to guide their actions in highly contextualized classroom settings. This form of practical knowledge entails, among other things, (a) knowledge of how to structure and represent academic content for direct teaching to students; (b) knowledge of the common conceptions, misconceptions, and difficulties that students encounter when learning particular content; and (c) knowledge of the specific teaching strategies that can be used to address students' learning needs in particular classroom circumstances. In the view of Shulman (and others), pedagogical content knowledge builds on other forms of professional knowledge, and is therefore a critical—and perhaps even the paramount—constitutive element in the knowledge base of teaching."

2. The RTTC and PTTC trainees thus share two scores in common (pedagogy score and total score); these are not likely to be comparable since they are based on different assessment metrics.

Bibliography

Darling-Hammond, Linda. 2002. "Defining 'Highly Qualified Teachers': What Does 'Scientifically Based Research' Actually Tell Us?" *Educational Researcher* 31 (9): 13–25.

Hill, Heather C., Deborah L. Ball, and Stephen G. Schilling. 2008. "Unpacking Pedagogical Content Knowledge: Conceptualizing and Measuring Teachers' Topic-Specific Knowledge of Students." *Journal for Research in Mathematics Education* 39 (4): 372–400.

Marcelo, Carlos. 2002. "Learning to Teach in the Knowledge Society: Literature Review." Paper commissioned by the World Bank and prepared for International Study on Learning to Teach in Secondary Schools.

Rowan, Brian, Stephen G. Schilling, Deborah L. Ball, and Robert Miller. 2001. *Measuring Teachers' Pedagogical Content Knowledge in Surveys: An Exploratory Study.* Philadelphia, PA: Consortium for Policy Research in Education, Ministry of Education, Youth and Sports.

Shulman, Lee S. 1986. "Those Who Understand: Knowledge Growth in Teaching." *Educational Researcher* 15 (2): 4–14.

World Bank. 2012a. "Teacher Training College Survey." World Bank, Washington, DC.

———. 2012b. "Teacher Survey." World Bank, Washington, DC.

CHAPTER 6

From Diagnosis to Reform: Three Policy Pillars to Raise Teaching Quality in Cambodia

Cambodian teaching quality faces major challenges. Low pay, low entry requirements, and low teacher trainee caliber make teaching an unattractive profession. Teacher preparation does not provide content mastery or exposure to interactive, student-centered pedagogical environments. Teacher performance is inhibited by ineffective incentives, an evaluation system that is disconnected from classroom realities, and a lack of opportunities to learn and share best-practice lessons with peers. With a bold reform agenda, Cambodia can get the most from its investments in teachers and bolster student learning.

We present three policy pillars to train, maintain, and motivate the Cambodian teaching workforce.

- The government needs to make teaching more attractive.
- The government must improve teacher preparation.
- The government must encourage stronger classroom performance.

Policy Pillar 1: Making Teaching More Attractive

Attracting more talented individuals to join the teaching ranks requires a coordinated policy response, tackling many interdependent factors in a holistic manner, including salaries and salary structure, the profession's status, and Teacher Training Center (TTC) selectivity. If salaries and prestige are adequate to attract top graduates and if instruction quality is high, then the TTCs will be able to impose stricter entry requirements. Conversely, without stricter entry requirements, the profession's status will not rise, even with more generous salaries. These interrelated elements require a harmonized policy framework, and several options are available to reform the current salary structure that would not increase its fiscal burden.

Make Salaries Attractive

Despite recent salary increases, the labor market is unfavorable for teachers, particularly female teachers. Regional comparisons underscore teachers' relatively low wages, and the earnings of a married teacher with two dependents is below the poverty line. Over the long term, higher salaries may be necessary to attract more talented candidates into teaching. Studies from around the world confirm that potential teachers care deeply about their salary levels as a teacher in comparison to other occupations (Boyd and others 2006; Dolton 1990; Wolter and Denzler 2003) and that competitive salaries attract more able candidates into teaching (Barber, Mourshed, and Whelan 2007; Figlio 1997; Hanushek, Kain, and Rivkin 1999; Leigh 2009).

A working group within the Ministry of Civil Service is considering short-term (2014), medium-term (2014–16), and long-term (2016 and beyond) compensation reform plans. These reforms include raising the minimum salary to $106 a month—a 28 percent increase—and the wage ceiling for the highest ranked civil servants to more than $150 a month—a 5 percent increase. The Ministry of Civil Service and the Ministry of Economy and Finance have calculated that this wage increase will cost the government approximately $100 million. The 2014 budget reflects these salary changes, which must be enacted responsibly and efficiently.

Some general principles may be useful to consider when reexamining salary structures. For fiscal sustainability purposes, public sector wage increases should be mindful of the pace of domestic revenue improvement. Wage increases should be set as part of human resource management within a broader civil service reform. Furthermore, it is advisable that key decisions on wage increases reflect various considerations: fiscal affordability, the need for human resource management policies for improving productivity, and expansion of equitable access to quality public services. Finally, policy makers considering the wage increases may also consider how an increased wage bill may affect other priority spending, in particular, outlays for maintenance that are critical for keeping the capital stock in decent shape.

Ensure On-Time Salary Payments

Teachers need to receive their full salaries on time. Salary delays averaging 10 days (nearly 2.5 months for bonuses) are a major grievance among teachers; nearly half of teachers never receive their full salaries. Such problems demotivate and frustrate teachers and may harm the profession's attractiveness even more than low starting salaries. The government could develop a system—perhaps using new technologies such as cell phones or the Internet or using the banking system (a plan which is under development through a joint committee)—to deliver teacher salaries in full and on time each month. Eliminating payment delays would effectively raise salaries without impacting the budget.

Such a development would assure teachers that policies to improve teaching will also benefit teachers.

Make TTC Entry Requirements Stricter and More Transparent

Raising salaries will only lead to higher quality teacher candidates if TTCs also impose more selective and transparent entry requirements. Low performance on external competency measures reveals deep weaknesses in teachers' core skills and shows that selectivity is a major issue. Unless performance improves, salary increases will only lead to higher paid low-quality teachers. International evidence on policies to recruit great teachers has identified "the intellectual caliber of the teaching force as a critical factor that takes education systems from good to great (Barber, Mourshed, and Whelan 2007)." Japan, the Republic of Korea, and Singapore restrict entrance to their national teacher training institutions very tightly.

The lack of transparency in TTC admissions also contributes to low teacher trainee caliber. The government must address this problem, as it constrains TTC selectivity, leads to cheating and absenteeism among trainees, and threatens teaching's professional ethos. Reforming entrance exam requirements and ensuring transparency in exam administration and scoring should be considered a high priority.

Provide Scholarships and Financial Aid for High-Performing Secondary Students

Many high-performing systems have used scholarships and financial incentives to attract top secondary school talent into teaching. Hong Kong SAR, China, and Singapore provide their teacher trainees with tuition waivers and large stipends (box 6.1). In the United Kingdom, science teacher trainees (who are in relatively short supply) receive scholarships to top universities, conditional on their teaching for three years after graduation. In Latin America,

---

Box 6.1 How Singapore Attracts Great Teachers

Singapore's National Institute of Education is the country's only teacher training institution. It produces Singapore's entire teaching workforce. Prospective teachers are carefully selected from the top one-third of the secondary school graduating class. In addition to high academic ability, students are assessed on the basis of their commitment to the profession and to serving diverse student bodies. Trainees receive monthly stipends throughout their education that are competitive with monthly salaries for recent graduates in other fields. They must commit to teaching for at least three years. Interest in teaching is developed early through teaching internships for high school students; there is also a system for midcareer entry.

Source: OECD 2010.

Colombia has recently rolled out an ambitious student loan program to attract high-performing students to teaching. Such targeted financial incentives—perhaps with higher stipends for top grade 12 exam scorers—may help Cambodia's teacher training system attract more top secondary graduates. But these strategies will probably only work if unfair and informal practices in TTC admissions is addressed.

Enforce the Prohibition on Private Tutoring

Widespread, unregulated private tutoring—outlawed in 2008—is harming the profession and undermining its public perception. It also allows the government to keep teacher salaries low by having families augment them. Tutoring lowers quality for many students in normal class sessions and may also encourage corrupt practices.

Policy Pillar 2: Improving Teacher Preparation

Embed Teacher Standards into Daily Classroom Practice in TTCs

Incorporating the teacher standards more widely into the TTC training program could help ensure teaching quality and coherence. The teacher standards provide a comprehensive statement of values, competencies, and expectations for teachers. But only half of TTCs have integrated the teacher standards into the curriculum. Less than 10 percent of provincial teacher training center (PTTC) trainers frequently use the teacher standards in their classes. More strikingly, less than 10 percent of regional teacher training center (RTTC) trainees are aware that the teacher standards exist. Even fewer have a written copy.

Incorporating the teacher standards into TTCs could significantly raise student achievement. A first step would be to disseminate copies of the teacher standards, particularly to trainers, and post them visibly in all TTC classrooms. Second, the teacher standards could be explicitly integrated into the TTC curriculum, preferably as their own required module. Third, TTC curricula should be reviewed and adjusted to ensure they reflect the expected competencies and behaviors.

Promote Peer Collaboration among Teacher Trainers and the Education System

Many teacher trainers report frustration with a lack of interaction with other teachers, input from school directors, and direction from the teacher training department. Nearly every RTTC trainer and roughly 90 percent of PTTC trainers report never or almost never visiting other TTC classrooms. Establishing a means for TTC trainees to interact, share, and receive support when needed would improve practice and motivation among TTC staff. Supporting TTC trainees to regularly upgrade their skills would bolster their confidence and provide exposure to more effective training. Peer collaboration is the hallmark of high-performing systems such as those in Japan (box 6.2) and Ontario, Canada.

Box 6.2 Peer Collaboration: Japan's Lesson Study

Japan's Lesson Study is a peer collaboration system where groups of teachers plan, deliver, observe, and discuss lessons with a particular pedagogic focus.

Teachers in the Lesson Study group work together in six phases. First, they agree on the Lesson Study's focus and the classroom techniques they aim to improve. Second, the group considers the learning needs of the class to be taught and collaboratively designs an innovative lesson or sequence of lessons using the chosen techniques. The planning specifies resources, teaching approaches, intended student activity, anticipated student responses, and outcomes. Third, one teacher agrees to teach the lesson and the remainder of the group observes closely how students react, how effectively they learn and make progress, and how well the lesson design meets students' needs and engages them in learning. Fourth, the group meets to review the lesson's effectiveness and share observations about its impact. They consider what worked, what needs to be adjusted, and what has been learned. Fifth, they revise and adjust the lesson based on the review.

They then repeat the Lesson Study, taking these revisions into account, with a different member of the group teaching and with a different class or group of students. This second lesson is reviewed for its effectiveness and impact on student learning.

Finally, the Lesson Study group considers what has been learned from the process and agrees on ways to share these findings within and beyond the department or school.

Source: OECD 2010.

Use Scripted Lessons to Promote Student-Centered Pedagogy in TTCs

Teacher trainers could use more student-centered techniques, such as giving students more opportunities to share their opinions; reducing the amount of time spent copying from the board; and asking more complex, challenging questions to ensure lesson comprehension.

Scripted approaches that use specific teaching strategies and accompanying materials to deliver well-defined daily curricula can help, especially since many Cambodian teacher trainers have low content and pedagogical content knowledge (PCK) mastery. These approaches provide teacher trainers with highly detailed instructions on what to cover in each lesson and how to present topics, incorporate learning materials, and assess student progress (Abadzi 2007). Teacher guides and student workbooks for these approaches have been particularly effective when teacher planning is weak, as demonstrated by a lack of lesson plans or homework assignments. These lesson scripts can be adjusted to solicit more student participation, improve classroom management, and reduce time-off-task—all issues needing attention in TTC classrooms (box 6.3).

Administer Competency Tests at the End of Teacher Training

Teacher trainers and trainees need to upgrade their content and PCK mastery substantially. Further, PCK elements should be introduced into the TTC curriculum. The government could consider standardized testing of teacher

> **Box 6.3 Scripted Approaches to Encourage Student-Centered Learning: Escuela Nueva in Vietnam**
>
> Vietnam recently adopted Colombia's international learning model (Escuela Nueva) to reform its education system and prepare its children better for the 21st century. The Escuela Nueva model, which depends heavily on detailed teacher scripts and student workbooks, shifts the focus from the teacher to the students, who use self-paced learning materials, tutor each other (cross-peer tutoring), draw on an enriched classroom learning environment, and work more in groups. To implement this shift, Vietnam provided group training in Escuela Nueva aims, concepts, materials, and methods; supported teacher visits to demonstration schools to see the model in action and learn from experienced teachers; provided ongoing teacher support through visits from master teachers; and delivered periodic professional development sessions to reinforce and extend teaching practice. After a successful pilot in 24 primary schools, Vietnam scaled the practice up to all 63 provinces.
>
> *Source:* World Bank staff reports.

skills and competencies, including PCK, as part of the exit exam to monitor and compare TTC training quality and identify talented teacher candidates to place at underperforming rural or remote schools. Many countries are shifting to such a competency-based approach. A new program in Brazil, for example, requires new candidate teachers to undergo an 80-hour training course in classroom dynamics—drawing largely on the Stallings method—after which they are observed and evaluated before their contracts are confirmed.

Increase the Quantity and Quality of Real Classroom Exposure in the Training Practicum

Cambodian teacher trainees are required to undertake only a very small amount (about 14 weeks) of assisted teaching during their first- and second-year practicum. Darling-Hammond and others' 2005 review of teacher preparation programs recommends that teacher trainees spend at least 30 weeks in the classroom practicing teaching. Boyd (2009) has shown that teaching practice is an extremely important part of training because teacher trainees then receive feedback. Cambodia could take steps to improve both quantity and quality of practical, experiential TTC learning. Rarely, if ever, does a teacher trainee in Cambodia watch him or herself on video or get observed and critiqued by seasoned, high-quality teachers. The current practicum may thus have only limited impact if teacher trainees are not given extensive opportunities to practice teaching and receive meaningful feedback to improve performance.

Include TTCs in the Postsecondary Quality Assurance Process

Trainees perform better than their trainers in math and PCK, and TTCs have no accreditation standards. A radical review of TTCs and trainer recruitment, selection, and preparation is urgently needed.

Cambodia could institute strong internal and external quality assurance procedures using its national quality assurance system, which is designed to monitor, certify, and improve tertiary education institutions and ensure their consistency with public policy goals. Integrating TTCs into the quality assurance system can enable them to perform institutional self-evaluation and access expert external evaluation and accreditation decisions, all based on quality criteria established by the Ministry with oversight authority. Adequate facilities, sufficient content and pedagogical content knowledge, and graduate competency assurance should inform TTC institutional reviews.

Policy Pillar 3: Encouraging Stronger Performance in the Classroom

Many of the policy levers to improve teacher preparation also apply to current teacher performance, particularly in teacher standards and peer collaboration. Even more urgent is reforming incentives.

Ensure that Teacher Standards Inform Classroom Practice

An urgent priority is to familiarize the entire teaching force with the teacher standards. Ministry of Education, Youth, and Sport (MoEYS) could ensure that every teacher has a written copy of the standards, that every school director posts them in a highly visible place in the school, that parents are informed about them, and that teachers can ask about the contents. It is recommended that information dissemination and training in the teacher standards explain in detail each of the competencies and expectations teachers are supposed to meet. For example, where would a rural Cambodian teacher go to "undertake professional reading and research to extend the range of knowledge to improve his/her teaching?" Such issues could be discussed among teacher themselves, perhaps as part of teacher technical meetings. These issues could also be discussed with parents and community members who could provide feedback to MoEYS on various measures of teacher performance (including attendance) through community score cards. A redoubled effort to raise awareness of the teacher standards needs to be better grounded in teachers' lives and resource constraints if the teacher standards are to take root in individual schools.

Promote Peer Collaboration through Strengthened Teacher Technical Meetings

Cambodia can leverage teacher technical meetings to promote more and better peer collaboration and further improve education quality. Student achievement in select subjects is higher in schools with more useful technical meetings. Sending expert facilitators, experienced teachers, or perhaps even TTC trainees to offer reviews on new materials, curricula, pedagogy, and best practice elsewhere could enhance such meetings. Introducing Lesson Study, discussed above, could also help (Fernandez 2002). Top-performing systems in other countries support teacher professional development through constant interaction and peer collaboration. In Finland, for example, teachers spend 40 percent less time in the classroom than the average Organisation for Economic Co-operation and Development (OECD) teacher; the rest of their time is spent in joint work on curricular review, lesson planning, and student assessment.

Improve Lesson Planning and Execution, Focusing on Student-Centered Learning

Action is recommended to improve schools' learning environment, including teacher–student instructional balance, time on-task, use of textbooks, and lesson planning. Lessons in which students listen passively, do individual seatwork, or copy from the blackboard correlate with lower student achievement. Depending on the lesson content and objective, teachers and blackboards may be at the center. But learning outcomes are higher when students are consistently given the chance to participate and immediately reinforce what they have been taught. So a better balance must be struck between delivering content and having students ask questions, participate actively, and lead.

Making teachers more aware of how lesson time is used is critical. Less time should be spent off-task. Effective use of textbooks and other instructional materials can also improve education quality. Lesson plans, currently used in less than half of all classrooms (66.2 percent in urban schools and only 35 percent in rural and remote schools), could be used much more widely.

Scripted lessons and demonstration lessons—in person or on video—should be included in in-service teacher training.

Place Teacher Standards at the Heart of Teacher Evaluation

The teacher standards provide an officially approved, uniform, and standardized format to monitor and evaluate teachers. Teacher standards–based evaluation would link more clearly to student learning and education quality than the current teacher evaluation format, which is based on a civil service assessment.

The government could adapt the broad concepts outlined in the teacher standards into more concrete measures in a revised evaluation instrument. Such a revision would catalyze a shift from civil servants awaiting promotion to teachers striving for incremental gains in instructional practice. Demonstrated competencies according to these adapted teacher standards could also inform promotion, monitoring, and supervision by the District Office of Education and school directors, thus aligning school visit criteria with formal evaluations. Making the teacher standards central to the TTC curriculum (as discussed previously) would connect teachers' preservice training to later career evaluations. Teachers who understand the evaluation system clearly and know what is required of them are more likely to respond positively to monitoring and evaluation.

A teacher standards–based evaluation system has many advantages. Comprehensive, technically valid evaluations with positive and negative consequences for teachers can improve teacher quality. They can hold teachers accountable for performance, make preservice education more relevant and efficient, and provide teachers with more targeted feedback. And they can inform a transition to more performance-based incentives.

Link Incentives to Performance and/or the Demonstrated Competencies

Integrating the teacher standards into the teacher evaluation system is the first step to matching incentives with performance. This step can "lay down the path for meritorious teacher placement and career advancement (Benveniste, Marshall, and Aranjo 2008)."

Raising bonus pay may motivate better performance and decompress the salary scale, both key to making teaching more attractive. Bonus pay programs typically give a one-time reward to teachers or schools for achieving specific results. Bonus pay can be awarded to teachers, for example, on the basis of demonstrated content mastery, PCK mastery, classroom management skills, instructional time use, or student performance. The bonus amount is crucial. To attract more talented teachers, financial rewards for teaching must meet a minimum threshold relative to the wages of comparable professions.

The education budget is underspent by around 15 percent, implying that education administrators have room to raise the nonbasic salary categories, such as functional and pedagogical allowances. Raising these salary incentives—now so insignificant that most teachers do not know they exist—and using them differently could motivate teachers to take on new roles, such as mentors (for TTC practical training and induction programs), inservice training coordinators, and innovation project leaders. This strategy would decompress the salary scale and establish a teaching career advancement path without affecting the basic salary or, therefore, the national budget.

But specific incentives for those who perform well on the teacher standards evaluation need not be limited to pay increases. They can also include opportunities for professional development and advanced training that can, in turn, lead to career advancement. Whatever the design, clear rewards for incremental improvements in actual teaching skills and enhanced student performance, instead of automatic promotion according to civil service logic, would help ensure that salary increases reward the most motivated and competent teachers.

Make Incentives to Work in Understaffed and Remote Areas More Effective

Cambodia must also improve its bonus pay scheme for working in understaffed and remote areas. Increasing the amount of bonuses, exploring in-kind incentives, and spreading awareness of these special payments would contribute to a better incentive scheme. Incentive reforms could also link explicitly to student achievement and support the best teachers.

The current system of incentives and bonuses does little to address imbalances in the teaching force or raise student achievement. One fundamental problem is that many teachers remain unaware of the remote area bonus pay scheme. It is not well advertised in TTCs. Another problem is that bonuses are perceived to be too small to attract enough recruits. The amounts are low, and payment is often severely delayed. Perhaps for this reason, only one in three trainees recruited from rural areas is willing to return.

Larger bonuses and on-time delivery are needed. In-kind payments should also be considered: many teachers are willing to receive these kinds of payments.

Involve Teachers in Reform

Enlisting teachers in clarifying teaching issues can make feedback more effective. Teachers who have a voice in reforms are more likely to implement them (Darling-Hammond 1997; Fullan and Miles 1992). To date, information about teaching issues has come from standardized surveys and large quantitative data sets such as the teacher survey. Rarely are survey results shared with teachers themselves to elicit further feedback. Yet such an exercise would help teachers understand their work in a wider national policy reform context and help the MoEYS understand the issues facing teachers. The teacher survey noted (a) a lack of information and communication technology use in TTCs and (b) isolation of young teachers, as well as a lack of information sharing. Finding innovative ways, aided by technology, to elicit teacher feedback and allow teachers to share their ideas, raise questions, and access key information (such as teacher standards and shared teaching materials) would create more active teacher cooperation in ongoing reform. Involving teachers and principals in operationalizing teacher standards would create more ownership over them and may help improve their use in the classroom.***

In 2009, Dalton McGuinty, the Premier of Ontario, Canada, famously summarized the urgency of investing in human capital.

> If you think about the world we live in today, it's a world where you can borrow your capital, copy your technology, and buy your natural resources. There is only one thing left on which to build your advantage, build a strong economy and society, and that is talent. That's the only competitive advantage nowadays.
>
> —Dalton McGuinty, Premier, Ontario, Canada, 2009

Quality teachers are at the heart of developing the talent of the next generation. They underpin the educational investments that will drive growth in Cambodia moving forward. They are essential to system strengthening and quality enhancement. They are at the crossroads of sectoral, service delivery, public financial management, and civil service reform. Virtually every other sphere of Cambodia's education system has undergone a sea change of reform over the last decade. Teacher management should be next.

Bibliography

Abadzi, Helen, ed. 2007. *Efficient Learning for the Poor: Insights from the Frontier of Cognitive Neuroscience*. Washington, DC: World Bank.

Barber, Michael, Mona Mourshed, and Fenton Whelan. 2007. "Improving Education in the Gulf: Educational Reform Should Focus on Outcomes, Not Inputs." In *The McKinsey Quarterly 2007 Special Edition: Reappraising the Gulf States*. London: McKinsey.

Benveniste, Luis, Jeffery Marshall, and M. Caridad Aranjo. 2008. *Teaching in Cambodia*. Washington, DC: World Bank.

Boyd, Donald. 2009. "Teacher Preparation and Student Achievement." *Education Evaluation and Policy Analysis* 31 (4): 416–40.

Boyd, Donald, Pamela Grossman, Hamilton Lankford, Susanna Loeb, and James Wyckoff. 2006. "How Changes in Entry Requirements Alter the Teacher Workforce and Affect Student Achievement." *Education Finance and Policy* 1 (2): 176–216.

Darling-Hammond, Linda. 1997. *Doing What Matters Most: Investing in Quality Teaching.* New York: The National Commission on Teaching and America's Future.

Darling-Hammond, Linda, Deborah J. Holtzman, Su Jin Gatlin, and Julian V. Heilig. 2005. "Does Teacher Preparation Matter? Evidence about Teacher Certification, Teach for America, and Teacher Effectiveness." *Education Policy Analysis Archives* 13 (42): 1–23.

Dolton, Peter J. 1990. "The Economics of UK Teacher Supply: The Graduate's Decision." *The Economic Journal* 100 (400): 91–104.

Fernandez, Clea. 2002. "Learning from Japanese Approaches to Professional Development: the Case of Lesson Study." *Journal of Teacher Education* 53 (5): 393–405.

Figlio, David N. 1997. "Teacher Salaries and Teacher Quality." *Economic Letters* 55 (2): 267–71.

Fullan, Michael G., and Matthew B. Miles. 1992. "Getting Reform Right: What Works and What Doesn't." *Phi Delta Kappan* 73 (10): 744–52.

Hanushek, Eric A., John F. Kain, and Steven G. Rivkin. 1999. "Do Higher Salaries Buy Better Teachers?" Working Paper 7082, National Bureau of Economic Research, Cambridge, MA.

Jann, Ben. 2008. "A Stata Implementation of the Blinder-Oaxaca Decomposition." *The Stata Journal* 8 (4): 453–79.

Leigh, Andrew. 2009. "Estimating Teacher Effectiveness from Two-Year Changes in Students' Test Scores." Discussion Paper 619, Research School of Economics, Centre for Economic Policy Research, Australian National University, Sydney.

OECD (Organisation for Economic Co-operation and Development). 2010. *Strong Performers and Successful Reformers in Education: Lessons from PISA for the United States.* Paris: OECD.

Vegas, Emiliana. 2005. *Incentives to Improve Teaching Lessons from Latin America.* Washington, DC: World Bank.

Wolter, Stefan C., and Stefan Denzler. 2003. *Wage Elasticity of the Teacher Supply in Switzerland.* Discussion Paper 733, Institute for the Study of Labor, Bonn, Germany.

APPENDIX A

SABER-Teachers Framework

Table A.1 SABER-Teacher Policy Goals in Cambodia

Policy goal	Description	SABER rating and analysis for Cambodia
Setting clear expectations for teachers	Setting clear expectations for student and teacher performance can guide teachers' daily work and ensure teaching coherence.	This policy goal was rated as "established" because expectations for students and teachers are clear, although teachers do not have adequate time to fulfill their duties.
Attracting the best into teaching	Talented people may be more inclined to become teachers if entry requirements, compensations, working conditions, and career opportunities are in line with other well-regarded professions.	This policy goal was rated as "established" because a selection process into teacher education exists. Compensation and teacher entrance should be studied more closely, however.
Preparing teachers	Provide the training teachers need to succeed in the classroom, including subject and pedagogic knowledge, classroom management, and teaching practice.	This goal, rated as "latent," received the lowest ranking among the eight policy goals. Teacher training programs do not include enough practical professional experience, and there are no induction programs to help smooth the transition into teaching.
Matching teacher skills with student needs	Ensure fair, appropriate distribution of teachers across various circumstances, regions, grades, and subjects.	This policy goal was rated as "emerging" because there are not enough monetary incentives for teachers to work in remote schools.
Leading teachers with strong principals	Strengthen school principals' capacity to act as instructional leaders as well as school managers. The more capable a school principal, the more she/he can attract and retain competent teachers.	This policy goal was rated as "established" because high entry requirements and posting incentives for school principals exist. But principals still have limited authority over teacher firing and promotion.
Monitoring teaching and learning	Monitor and assess teacher and student performance.	This policy goal was rated as "established" because student assessments occur annually in selected grades and because teacher performance is regularly evaluated along multiple criteria. Further research can determine whether these initiatives are followed through.

table continues next page

Table A.1 SABER-Teacher Policy Goals in Cambodia *(continued)*

Policy goal	Description	SABER rating and analysis for Cambodia
Supporting teachers to improve instruction	Put in place a support system for teachers to improve instruction, analyzing specific challenges and developing solutions, including having access to information about best practices.	This policy goal was rated as "emerging" because teacher performance and student learning data are not used to inform teaching and learning. Professional development is also not available for all primary and secondary teachers.
Motivating teachers to perform	Set adequate incentives to provide effective teaching. The more aligned incentives are with the behaviors and outcomes they want to elicit, the more likely teachers will pursue them.	This policy goal is evaluated as "emerging" because few incentive structures focus on motivating top performance.

Note: SABER = Systems Approach for Better Results.

APPENDIX B

Oaxaca-Blinder Decomposition Methodology

Gross (Unadjusted) Wage Differentials

One way to measure teachers' opportunity cost is to compare average gross wages of teachers ($\overline{W}_T$) and other professionals ($\overline{W}_P$). The proportional (average) wage differential between them is given by the following:

$$G_{TP} = (\overline{W}_T/\overline{W}_P) - 1 \tag{B.1}$$

which is approximately equal to the log wage differential:

$$G_{TP} = \ln(G_{TP} + 1) = \ln(\overline{W}_T) - \ln(\overline{W}_P) \tag{B.2}$$

This wage difference is sensitive to the definition of the comparative group. The gross wage differential can stem from differences in endowments or returns. To use it to measure teachers' opportunity cost, we must compare teachers with individuals with similar human capital endowments.

Conditional (Adjusted) Wage Differentials

In competitive labor markets, wages equal the value of the marginal productivity of labor, that is, the wage is the function of workers' endowments of productive human capital and the returns of those endowments in the labor market. Gross wage differentials reflect differences in both endowments and returns. The part of the wage difference that can be attributed to different returns is the conditional (adjusted) wage differential.

If we suppose that the average wage of teachers and other professionals without any difference in returns to their respective endowments is $\overline{W}_{T0}$ and $\overline{W}_{P0}$, respectively, we can write the part of the (average) gross wage differential attributable to endowment differences follows:

$$Q_{TP} = (\overline{W}_{T0}/\overline{W}_{P0}) - 1 \tag{B.3}$$

Accordingly, the conditional (average) wage differential will be given by the difference between the gross and the productivity wage differentials:

$$D_{TP} = \frac{[(\overline{W}_T/\overline{W}_P)-(\overline{W}_{T0}/\overline{W}_{P0})]}{(\overline{W}_{T0}/\overline{W}_{P0})} \qquad (B.4)$$

The gross wage differential (G_{TP}) can thus be decomposed into two: endowment differences, Q_{TP}, and differences in labor market return, D_{TP}. From equation 4, we can write the aggregate difference as (Vegas 2005):

$$\ln(G_{TP}+1) = \ln(Q_{TP}+1) + \ln(D_{TP}+1) \qquad (B.5)$$

Oaxaca-Blinder Decomposition

An alternative formulation is a Mincer regression equation:

$$W_t = X_t \beta_t + \xi_t \qquad (B.6)$$

where $t \in (P, T)$; W_t is monthly wage; X_t is for vector human capital endowment indicators such as education, potential experience, location, and gender; and ξ_t is the error term with $E(\xi_t) = 0$.

To decompose the gross (unadjusted) difference between the mean monthly income of teachers and other professionals, that is, $\overline{W}_T - \overline{W}_P$, into endowment differences, coefficient differences (labor market return), and their interactions, we write the Oaxaca-Blinder decomposition equation as:

$$\overline{W}_T - \overline{W}_P = (\overline{X}_T - \overline{X}_P)'\beta_P + \overline{X}_{P'}(\beta_T - \beta_P) + [(\overline{X}_T - \overline{X}_P)]'(\beta_T - \beta_P) \qquad (B.7)$$

where $\overline{X}_t$ is mean of the vector of endowments for $t \in (P, T)$.

Equation 7 decomposes the gross difference in mean monthly income into three components: $\overline{W}_T - \overline{W}_P = E + C + I$. The first component, $E = (\overline{X}_T - \overline{X}_P)'\beta_P$, is a measure of difference in monthly income explained by endowment differences between teachers and other professionals. The second component, $C = \overline{X}_P'(\beta_T - \beta_P)$, measures the difference in labor market return. The third component, $I = [(\overline{X}_T - \overline{X}_P)]'(\beta_T - \beta_P)$, accounts for the simultaneous existence of coefficient and endowment differences between teachers and other professionals.

In the threefold decomposition, we use other professionals as a reference group and hence β_P in the first component. This entails a careful selection of a similar comparable group, that is, a group with similar endowments as teachers. An alternative approach in the labor market discrimination literature is to use a twofold decomposition by using a nondiscriminatory coefficient vector, β^*, generated through some combination of β_P and β_T, instead of just using β_P. Accordingly, we can rewrite equation 7 as follows:

$$\overline{W}_T - \overline{W}_P = (\overline{X}_T - \overline{X}_P)'\beta^* + \overline{X}_P'(\beta_T - \beta_P) + [(\overline{X}_T - \overline{X}_P)]'(\beta_T - \beta_P) \qquad (B.8)$$

Now we have two components: income differences explained by endowment differences, $E = (\overline{X}_T - \overline{X}_P)' \beta^*$, and unexplained income differences, $\overline{X}_P' (\beta_T - \beta_P) + [(\overline{X}_T - \overline{X}_P)]' (\beta_T - \beta_P)$. The second component is usually attributed to labor market discrimination, that is, differences in labor market return faced by teachers and other professionals.[1]

Note

1. The unexplained income difference may also stem from unobserved differences between teachers and other professionals, such as differences in ability (Jann 2008).

Bibliography

Jann, Ben. 2008. "The Blinder-Oaxaca Decomposition for Linear Regression Models." *The Stata Journal* 8 (4): 453–79.

Vegas, Emiliana. 2005. *Incentives to Improve Teaching: Lessons from Latin America*. Washington, DC: World Bank.

APPENDIX C

Tables: Teacher Wage and Income

Table C.1 Wage and Other Costs in Recurrent MoEYS Funding, 2010–13

Variable	2010	2011	2012	2013
Total recurrent education expenditure (millions of riel)	824,879.0	950,184.70	1,046,418.60	1,165,414.90
Personnel cost (% of recurrent)	73.9	72.3	72.3	72.3
Nonpersonnel cost % of recurrent)	26.1	27.7	27.7	27.7

Source: MoEYS 2010.
Note: MoEYS = Ministry of Education, Youth, and Sport.

Table C.2 Determinants of Labor Income in Cambodia: Teachers versus Other Professionals, 2007–11 (Dependent Variable: Logarithm of Monthly Earnings)

	Teachers		Other professionals	
Explanatory variables	Coefficient	t	Coefficient	t
Years of schooling	0.02	1.93***	0.06	10.06***
With professional qualification (certificate)	0.12	0.02	−0.04	−0.90
With professional qualification (degree)	0.39	5.02***	0.14	3.46***
Potential experience	5.90	4.23***	5.13	6.16***
Potential experience squared	−0.76	−3.85***	−0.79	−6.65***
Female	−0.11	−3.13***	−0.02	−0.58
Married	0.07	1.65*	0.07	2.26***
Urban	0.16	4.43***	0.27	7.39***
Phnom Penh	0.11	1.95***	0.34	10.59***
Constant	0.80	0.32	3.56	2.46***
R-Square	0.27		0.27	
F	25.25***		158.35***	

Source: National Institute of Statistics 2007–11.
Significance level: * = 10 percent, ** = 5 percent, *** = 1 percent.

Table C.3 Oaxaca-Blinder Decomposition of Male and Female Teachers' Income (Dependent Variable: Logarithm of Monthly Earnings)

Overall	Threefold (equation 7)		Discrimination (equation 8)	
	Coefficient	z	Coefficient	z
Group 1: Male	12.641	429.54***		
Group 2: Female	12.477	471.00***		
Differences	0.165	4.16**	0.165	4.16***
Endowments	0.035	1.51		
Coefficients	0.096	2.57*		
Interaction	0.033	1.23		
"Explained"			0.054	2.35**
"Unexplained"			0.110	3.14***

Source: National Institute of Statistics 2007–11.
Significance level: * = 10 percent, ** = 5 percent, *** = 1 percent.

Table C.4 List of Other Professionals Compared with Teachers in Cambodia

Administration professionals	Medical doctors
Administrative and specialized secretaries	Mining, manufacturing, and construction supervisors
Architects, planners, surveyors, and designers	Numerical clerks
Armed forces occupations	Nursing and midwifery associate professionals
Artistic, cultural, and culinary associate professionals	Nursing and midwifery professionals
Authors, journalists, and linguists	Other clerical support workers
Business services agents	Other health associate professionals
Business services and administration managers	Other health professionals
Client information workers	Other services managers
Creative and performing artists	Paramedical practitioners
Database and network professionals	Physical and earth science professionals
Electrotechnology engineers	Physical and engineering science technicians
Engineering professionals (excluding electrotechnology)	Process control technicians
Finance professionals	Production managers in agriculture, forestry, and fisheries
Financial and mathematical associate professionals	Professional services managers
General office clerks	Regulatory government associate professionals
Hotel and restaurant managers	Retail and wholesale trade managers
Information and communications technology operations and user support technicians	Sales and purchasing agents and brokers
Information and communications technology service managers	Sales, marketing, and development managers
Keyboard operators	Sales, marketing, and public relations professionals
Legal professionals	Secretaries (general)
Legal, social, and religious associate professionals	Ship and aircraft controllers and technicians
Legislators and senior officials	Social and religious professionals

table continues next page

Table C.4 List of Other Professionals Compared with Teachers in Cambodia *(continued)*

Librarians, archivists, and curators	Software and applications developers and analysts
Life science professionals	Sports and fitness workers
Life science technicians and related associate professionals	Telecommunications and broadcasting technicians
Managing directors and chief executives	Tellers, money collectors, and related clerks
Manufacturing, mining, construction, and distribution managers	Traditional and complementary medicine associate professionals
Material-recording and transport clerks	Traditional and complementary medicine professionals
Mathematicians, actuaries, and statisticians	Veterinarians
Medical and pharmaceutical technicians	Veterinary technicians and assistants

Source: National Institute of Statistics 2007–11.

Table C.5 List of Other Professionals Compared with Teachers in Thailand and Vietnam

Thailand	Vietnam
Mining and quarrying	Agriculture, forestry, and fishing
Manufacturing	Mining and quarrying
Electricity, gas, and water supply	Manufacturing
Construction	Electricity, gas, steam, and air conditioning supply
Wholesale and retail trade, repair of motor vehicles and motorcycles, personal and household goods	Water supply, sewerage, waste management, and remediation activities
Hotel and restaurants	Construction
Transport, storage, and communication	Wholesale and retail trade, repair of motor vehicles, and motorcycles
Financial intermediation	Transportation and storage
Real estate, renting, and business activities	Accommodation and food service activities
Public administration and defense, compulsory social security	Information and communication
Education	Financial, banking, and insurance activities
Health and social work	Real estate activities
Other community, social, and personal service activity	Professional, scientific, and technical activities
Private households with employed persons	Administrative and support service activities
Extraterritorial organizations and bodies	Communist Party, sociopolitical organizations, public administration and defense, compulsory social security
Unknown	*Education and training*
	Human health and social work activities
	Arts, entertainment, and recreation
	Other service activities
	Hired domestic help
	Activities of international organizations and agencies

Source: Ministry of Information and Communication Technology 2011 (Thailand); Ministry of Planning and Investment 2012 (Vietnam).

Bibliography

Ministry of Education, Youth, and Sport (Cambodia). 2010. "Education Strategic Plan 2009–13." Phnom Penh, Government of Cambodia.

Ministry of Information Communication (Cambodia). Various years. "The Labour Force Survey." National Statistics Office, Phnom Penh, Government of Cambodia.

Ministry of Planning and Investment (Vietnam). "The Labour Force Survey." General Statistics Office, Hanoi, Government of Vietnam.

National Institute of Statistics. 2007–11. *Cambodia Socio-Economic Survey.* Phnom Penh: Government of Cambodia, Ministry of Planning.

APPENDIX D

Scatterplots

Figure D.1 Khmer Achievement and Active Instruction (As Share of Total Time), School Averages

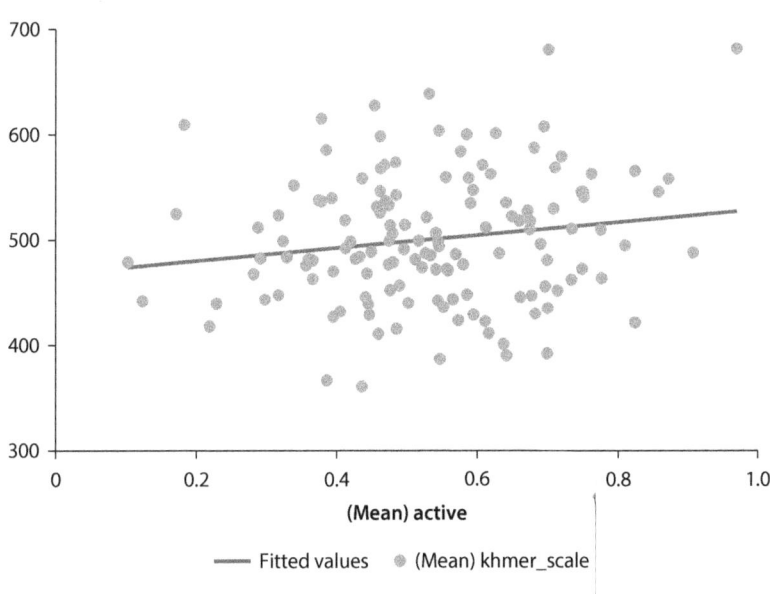

Source: World Bank 2012.
Note: Slope = 0.16, R2 = 0.02, sig. = 0.06.

Figure D.2 Math Achievement and Active Instruction (As Share of Total Time), School Averages

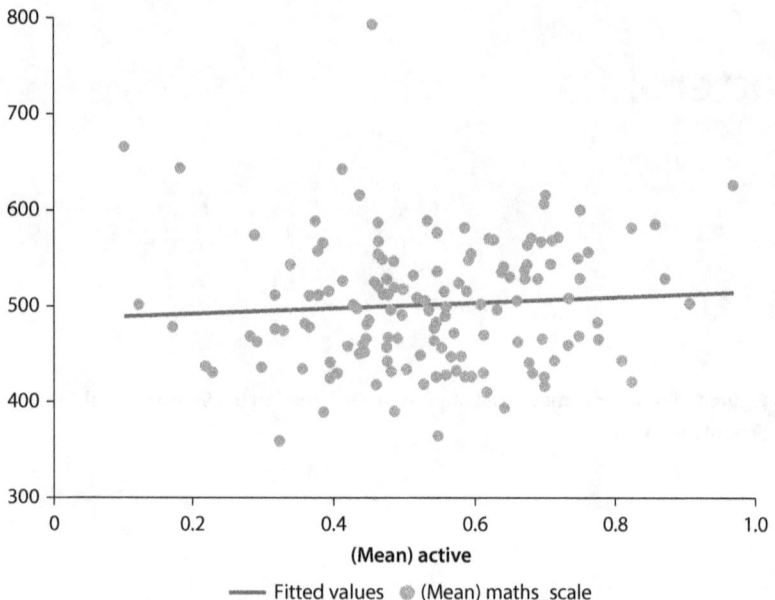

Source: World Bank 2012.
Note: Slope = 0.07, R2 = 0.00, sig. = 0.40.

Bibliography

World Bank. 2012. "Teacher Training College Survey." World Bank, Washington, DC.

APPENDIX E

Multivariate Results

Table E.1 Multivariate Analysis of Student Achievement: Baseline Model Results

Variable	Khmer			Math		
	HLM	OLS weight	OLS	HLM	OLS weight	OLS
Child/family						
Child age (years)	1.01	0.45	4.12*	2.22*	1.32	4.65**
	(0.89)	(0.42)	(2.11)	(2.00)	(0.61)	(2.64)
Female	−9.70**	−15.63**	−11.64**	−4.71+	−10.24*	−4.96
	(−3.74)	(−3.61)	(−3.14)	(−1.76)	(−1.93)	(−1.32)
Number of siblings	−1.66*	−0.79	−1.41+	−1.72*	−2.50*	−2.69**
	(−2.11)	(−0.80)	(−1.71)	(−2.23)	(−2.32)	(−2.83)
SES (factor)	13.03**	15.98**	13.68**	9.81**	10.55**	10.00**
	(5.11)	(5.48)	(4.58)	(3.91)	(4.02)	(2.99)
School fees (pct.)	0.22*	0.25+	0.43**	0.13	0.16	0.33*
	(2.34)	(1.78)	(2.71)	(1.27)	(0.64)	(2.04)
Number of G1–G3 repetition episodes	−3.16	−3.46	−0.48	−4.08*	−4.57	−1.06
	(−1.57)	(−0.61)	(−0.13)	(−2.07)	(−1.13)	(−0.32)
Absences						
1–2 absences	−6.32	−8.13	−10.19+	−3.13	−9.73	−4.17
	(−1.42)	(−1.18)	(−1.77)	(−0.71)	(−0.89)	(−0.61)
3–5 absences	−9.13*	−10.88+	−11.00*	−8.39*	−3.55	4.76
	(−2.05)	(−1.77)	(−1.98)	(−1.93)	(−0.38)	(−0.67)
6–10 absences	−18.90**	−7.83	−19.28*	−14.17**	−20.62	−9.59
	(−3.20)	(−0.79)	(−2.34)	(−2.71)	(−1.04)	(−1.05)
11–20 absences	−17.53*	−28.29*	−20.94*	−18.62*	−28.18	−13.77
	(−2.00)	(−2.41)	(−2.20)	(−2.18)	(−1.14)	(−1.13)
More than 20	−11.73	−6.51	−14.16	−4.49	16.69	6.00
	(−0.95)	(−0.47)	(−1.45)	(−0.37)	(0.97)	(0.42)
School/community						
SES average (factor)	14.53	15.86*	15.52+	3.55	−5.71	4.93
	(1.62)	(2.10)	(1.73)	(0.32)	(−0.28)	(0.44)
Rural	−27.99+	−18.29	−20.81	−25.65	−27.92	−22.93
	(−1.62)	(−1.00)	(−1.39)	(−1.21)	(−1.11)	(−1.49)
Total enrollment	0.07	0.06**	0.06*	0.11*	0.13	0.10
	(1.50)	(2.73)	(2.37)	(1.97)	(1.12)	(1.15)

table continues next page

Table E.1 Multivariate Analysis of Student Achievement: Baseline Model Results *(continued)*

	Khmer			Math		
Variable	HLM	OLS weight	OLS	HLM	OLS weight	OLS
Sample size (number)	3,606	3,606	3,606	3,606	3,606	3,606
Random effects	632.0**	—	—	982.4**	—	—
Explained variance (R^2)	—	0.30	0.16	—	0.22	0.11

Source: World Bank 2012a.
Note: HLM refers to random effects model ("xtmixed" command in Stata Version 12); OLS models are with and without survey weights. Robust standard errors are used in all estimations (*t*–statistics in parentheses). Coefficients are not standardized. Additional variables include controls for mother's education. SES = socioeconomic status; — = not applicable.
Significance level: * = 0.05, ** = 0.01, + = 0.10.

Table E.2 Multivariate Analysis of Student Achievement: Teacher Questionnaire Variables

	Subject	
Variable	Khmer	Maths
Teacher pays facilitation fee	−22.39	−17.65
	(−1.54)	(−0.95)
Teacher pay delays	27.17+	9.80
	(1.88)	(0.54)
Teacher has had other job	−19.25	−52.70**
	(−1.24)	(−2.70)
Usefulness of teacher technical meetings	31.45*	9.42
	(2.03)	(0.48)
School has system for teachers to visit other classrooms	−17.07	−3.75
	(−1.06)	(−0.20)
Frequency of director visits to classroom	2.29	5.17
	(0.36)	(0.65)
Teacher degree of understanding of evaluation system	7.58	24.63**
	(1.03)	(2.66)
Teacher incorporation of standards	33.98*	23.21
	(2.11)	(1.15)
Amount of bonus pay	−20.30	−11.33
	(−1.39)	(−0.62)
Teacher inservice training in last year	30.99	55.95
	(1.01)	(1.41)
Receiving remote deployment incentive	−25.91*	−23.64
	(−2.03)	(−1.54)
Receiving double shift incentive	−2.36	−5.78
	(−0.18)	(−0.36)
Natural log of teacher salary	11.89	33.81
	(0.44)	(−0.99)
Teacher is from other province	18.90	−23.14
	(0.70)	(0.69)
Interaction: Teacher from other province remote incentive	34.77	66.59
	(0.82)	(1.25)

table continues next page

Table E.2 Multivariate Analysis of Student Achievement: Teacher Questionnaire Variables *(continued)*

	Subject	
Variable	Khmer	Maths
Sample size (number)	3,513	3,513
Random effects	481.2**	827.1**

Source: World Bank 2012a.
Note: All models are HLM (see table E1) with robust standard errors (*t*-statistics in parentheses). Coefficients are not standardized. All models include the child and family background variables analyzed in table E1.
Significance level: * = 0.05, ** = 0.01, + = 0.10.

Table E.3 Multivariate Analysis of Student Achievement: Director Questionnaire Variables

	Subject	
Variable	Khmer	Math
Frequency of meetings with DOE	0.62	−1.24
	(0.61)	(−0.97)
Teacher training/PD	16.13	1.92
	(1.36)	(0.13)
Participation on school support committee	−21.77	−18.16
	(−1.16)	(−0.77)
Frequency of DOE visits	5.52	6.01
	(1.22)	(1.05)
Frequency of teacher evaluations	−0.22	0.32
	(−0.65)	(0.76)
Knowledge of teacher standards	−13.77	−11.34
	(−1.52)	(−1.00)
Actions taken with poorly performing teachers		
Given written notification	8.69	7.24
	(0.73)	(0.48)
Assign professional development	1.58	6.45
	(0.14)	(0.45)
Assign mentor	7.93	−4.71
	(0.82)	(−0.39)
Report to DOE	−53.63*	−21.01
	(−2.03)	(−0.67)
Fire teacher	26.13	3.12
	(0.70)	(0.07)
Director age	0.74	0.40
	(1.58)	(0.67)
Director education	4.86	7.26
	(1.26)	(1.50)
Director is female	28.14*	36.83*
	(2.12)	(2.22)
Sample size (number)	3,606	3,606
Random effects	529.9**	907.2**

Source: World Bank 2012a.
Note: All models are HLM (see table E1) with robust standard errors (*t*-statistics in parentheses). Coefficients are not standardized. All models include the child and family background variables analyzed in table E1. DOE = District Office of Education; PD = professional development.
Significance level: * = 0.05, ** = 0.01.

Table E.4 Multivariate Analysis of Student Achievement: Teacher and Student Attendance Observations

	Teacher attendance		Student attendance	
Variable	Khmer	Math	Khmer	Math
Teacher attendance (%)	−4.52	3.16	—	—
	(−0.16)	(0.09)		
Teacher years of study	−3.20	−2.98	—	—
	(−0.77)	(−0.58)		
Teacher years of training	−4.10	−7.19	—	—
	(−0.38)	(−0.54)		
Teacher years of experience	−1.38+	−2.29*	—	—
	(−1.64)	(−2.22)		
Student attendance (%)	—	—	−1.24	−39.52
			(−0.03)	(−0.87)
Has textbook (%)	—	—	24.55	3.50
			(1.23)	(0.14)
Has purchased textbook (%)	—	—	8442	89.10
			(1.60)	(1.37)
Sample size (number)	3,583	3,583	3,581	3,581
Random effects	603.2**	979.0**	611.6	1008.1**

Source: World Bank 2012a.
Notes: All models are HLM (see table E1) with robust standard errors (*t*-statistics in parentheses). Coefficients are not standardized. All models include the child and family background variables analyzed in table E1.
— = Variable is not included in this estimation of the statistical analysis.
Significance level: * = 0.05, ** = 0.01, + = 0.10.

Table E.5 Multivariate Analysis of Student Achievement: Classroom Observations

	Khmer		Mathematics	
Variable	(1)	(2)	(1)	(2)
Teacher takes attendance	11.47	—	14.32	—
	(1.03)		(1.01)	
Teacher has written lesson plan	−4.22	—	−4.11	—
	(−0.38)		(−0.30)	
Cleanliness of classroom	−2.41	—	15.03	—
	(−0.22)		(1.09)	
Use of teaching aids	3.83	—	7.33	—
	(0.28)		(0.42)	
Use of textbooks	28.78+	—	3.58	—
	(1.91)		(0.57)	
Use of individual questions	−0.57**	—	−0.39	—
	(−2.92)		(−1.59)	
Students ask teacher questions	0.62	—	6.60	—
	(0.04)		(0.37)	
Use of group work	9.74	—	1.09	—
	(0.81)		(0.67)	
Teacher monitoring of class	5.45	—	−20.93	—
	(0.32)		(−0.97)	

table continues next page

Table E.5 Multivariate Analysis of Student Achievement: Classroom Observations *(continued)*

	Khmer		Mathematics	
Variable	(1)	(2)	(1)	(2)
Teacher use of blackboard	7.59	—	11.41	—
	(1.31)		(1.55)	
Stallings category summaries				
Passive instruction	—	−24.71	—	−17.24
		(−0.92)		(−0.51)
Management	—	12.05	—	19.67
		(1.20)		(1.57)
Off-topic	—	−11.61*	—	−65.86
		(−1.91)		(−0.86)
Sample size (number)	3,552	3,552	3,552	3,552
Random effects	567.7**	603.6**	966.2**	992.8**

Source: World Bank 2012a.
Notes: All models are HLM (see table E1) with robust standard errors (*t*-statistics in parentheses). Coefficients are not standardized. Excluded category for Stallings category summaries is active instruction. All models include the child and family background variables analyzed in table E1. — = Variable is not included in this estimation of the statistical analysis.
Significance level: * = 0.05, ** = 0.01, + = 0.10.

Table E.6 Multivariate Analysis of Student Achievement: Teaching-Learning Environment (Student Interview)

	Khmer					Mathematics				
Variable	(1)	(2)	(3)	(4)	(5)	(1)	(2)	(3)	(4)	(5)
Teacher gets angry	−3.50	—	—	—	—	−6.45*	—	—		
	(−1.11)					(−2.09)				
School average (angry)	2.05	—	—	—	—	21.39	—	—		
	(0.17)					(1.42)				
Teacher gives opportunity to participate	—	4.24	—	—	—	—	5.49*	—		
		(1.47)					(1.95)			
School average (opportunity)	—	−3.97	—	—	—	—	1.12	—		
		(−0.37)					(0.08)			
Teacher provides help	—	—	−1.76	—	—	—	—	4.01		
			(−0.60)					(1.41)		
School average (help)	—	—	6.77	—	—	—	—	5.28		
			(0.61)					(0.39)		
Teacher sends to blackboard	—	—	—	6.40*	—	—	—	—	4.73+	
				(2.32)					(1.76)	
School average (blackboard)	—	—	—	−0.88	—	—	—	—	1.63	
				(−0.07)					(0.11)	
Teacher uses multiple choice questions	—	—	—	—	2.06	—	—	—	—	3.24
					(0.70)					(1.23)

table continues next page

Table E.6 Multivariate Analysis of Student Achievement: Teaching-Learning Environment (Student Interview) *(continued)*

	Khmer					Mathematics				
Variable	(1)	(2)	(3)	(4)	(5)	(1)	(2)	(3)	(4)	(5)
School average (multiple choice)	—	—	—	—	8.61 (0.77)	—	—	—	—	14.34 (1.05)
Sample size	3,552	3,552	3,552	3,552	3,552	3,552	3,552	3,552	3,552	3,552
Random effects	631**	631**	630**	626**	619**	1,029**	1,031**	1,029**	1,028**	1,016**

Source: World Bank 2012a.
Notes: All models are HLM (see table E1) with robust standard errors (*t*-statistics in parentheses). Coefficients are not standardized. All models include the child and family background variables analyzed in table E1. — = Variable is not included in this estimation of the statistical analysis.
Significance level: * = 0.05, ** = 0.01, + = 0.10.

Table E.7 Multivariate Analysis of Student Achievement: Teacher Mathematics Knowledge

	Khmer					Mathematics				
Variable	(1)	(2)	(3)	(4)	(5)	(1)	(2)	(3)	(4)	(5)
Overall mathematics knowledge	−15.69 (−0.56)	—	—	—	—	−5.58 (−0.16)	—	—	—	—
By component										
Content knowledge	—	−8.39 (−0.22)	−17.77 (−0.74)	—	—	—	−22.88 (−0.45)	−17.38 (−0.58)	—	—
TIMSS items	—	−20.35 (−0.65)	—	−19.45 (−0.37)	—	—	−20.89 (−0.54)	—	−16.52 (−0.32)	—
Sample size	3,606	3,606	3,606	3,606	3,606	3,606	3,606	3,606	3,606	3,606
Random effects	629**	622**	627**	633**	632**	1303**	1,018**	1030**	1033**	1031**

Source: World Bank 2012a.
Note: All models are HLM (see table E1) with robust standard errors (*t*-statistics in parentheses). Coefficients are not standardized. All models include the child and family background variables analyzed in table E1. TIMSS = Trends in Mathematics and Science Study; — = Variable is not included in this estimation of the statistical analysis.
Significance level: * = 0.05, ** = 0.01, + = 0.10.

Bibliography

World Bank. 2012a. Teacher Survey, World Bank, Washington, DC.

———. 2012b. Teacher Training College Survey, World Bank, Washington, DC.

Environmental Benefits Statement

The World Bank Group is committed to reducing its environmental footprint. In support of this commitment, the Publishing and Knowledge Division leverages electronic publishing options and print-on-demand technology, which is located in regional hubs worldwide. Together, these initiatives enable print runs to be lowered and shipping distances decreased, resulting in reduced paper consumption, chemical use, greenhouse gas emissions, and waste.

The Publishing and Knowledge Division follows the recommended standards for paper use set by the Green Press Initiative. Whenever possible, books are printed on 50 percent to 100 percent postconsumer recycled paper, and at least 50 percent of the fiber in our book paper is either unbleached or bleached using Totally Chlorine Free (TCF), Processed Chlorine Free (PCF), or Enhanced Elemental Chlorine Free (EECF) processes.

More information about the Bank's environmental philosophy can be found at http://crinfo.worldbank.org/wbcrinfo/node/4.